Correctional Law
for the
Correctional Officer

3rd Edition

William C. Collins, J.D.

344.035
C713c

Printed in the United States of America by Victor Graphics, Baltimore, Md.

For information on publications and videos available from ACA, contact our worldwide web home page at: http://www.corrections.com/aca

ISBN - 1-56991-132-0

This publication may be ordered from:
American Correctional Association
4380 Forbes Boulevard
Lanham, Maryland 20706-4322
1-800-222-5646

Library of Congress Cataloging-in-Publication Data

Collins, William C., 1944-
    Correctional law for the correctional officer /
        William C. Collins.–3rd ed.
        p. cm.
        ISBN 1-56991-132-0 (pbk.)
        1. Correctional law–United States. 2. Prisoners–Legal status, laws, etc.–United States.
      3.Correctional personnel–Legal status, laws, etc.–United States. I.
        Title.

    KF9728.Z9 C654 2001
    344.73'035–dc21   00-054842

Contents

Continued on the next page

Foreword

Correctional law continues to evolve. It is important for correctional staff to understand what the law says and what rights both inmates and staff have under it. By understanding the basics of the law, staff can avoid many potential problems and the court's scrutiny over conditions of confinement. In this book, readers will learn about legal liabilities and some of the complex areas of the law including searches and seizures, access to the courts, use of force, punishment, health concerns such as AIDS and suicide, questions of religion, mail, and visitation. In fact, the section on use of force has been expanded in this edition to meet the concerns of those in the field who must make life and death decisions.

The third edition of this popular book is an easy-to-read guide to correctional law. Each chapter has questions and answers so that readers can test their understanding of what they have read.

This book is an excellent addition to, not a replacement for, a thorough and ongoing training program for correctional staff. William Collins, a well-respected lawyer and writer, provides a national perspective and leaves it up to the state or locality to provide correct information that meets its regional concerns. Readers should consult with legal counsel regarding specific situations or further developments in correctional law.

James A. Gondles, Jr., CAE
Executive Director
American Correctional Association

I.
Introduction

This book is designed for the correctional officer. It describes, in a general way, many of the legal issues that the officer may face while working in corrections. Many of these issues relate to inmates, but some also focus on the officer and the officer's rights.

This handbook is for the correctional officer working in an adult prison or jail. It does not address legal issues that may arise in juvenile institutions or programs. While there has been a great deal of litigation about adult institutions, there have been relatively few lawsuits about conditions or practices in juvenile facilities. However, many of the fundamental principles discussed here would apply to juvenile facilities and programs.

No one working in corrections can avoid dealing with legal issues from time to time. Much of what goes on in a prison or jail today is governed by legal rules, which may come from state or federal statutes or state and federal constitutions. These rules may be enforced by a court. We hope that this handbook will increase the officer's understanding of the present law and the role of law and the courts in corrections.

The Role of the Correctional Officer

The role of the correctional officer has outgrown simply providing custody. The individual officer directly can affect the lives of the inmates. Some researchers believe the line officer is the most influential correctional employee in an inmate's life and is in a critical position to assist with the positive changes expected of the inmate. The officer also is responsible for carrying out the policies and rules of the correctional agency. The extent to which an institution abides by its own rules (and in turn complies with the requirements of statutes and the Constitution and state constitutions) depends a great deal on the correctional officer.

There are two types of lawsuits inmates file. In the first, the attack is on general policies or conditions in the institution. This type of suit often does not directly challenge any actions by individual officers, although its outcome may affect the officer's job. The second type of suit directly attacks actions (or failure to take actions) of the officer, often claiming the officer failed to follow the policies and procedures of the institution in a way that violated the rights of the inmate. (The person who files a lawsuit is known as the *plaintiff*. The person the suit is against is known as the *defendant*.)

Policies and procedures, post orders, and other written job directives that generally tell an officer what is expected are the officer's best source of law since those rules often are written to comply with statutory or constitutional requirements.

The Role and Function of the Courts

Courts play a unique role in our system of government and in the criminal justice system. Like police and correctional agencies, courts play an active role in controlling crime, determining guilt or innocence, and imposing sentences. But the courts also must perform a separate and distinct function: enforcing the requirements of the Constitution for government agencies and employees on behalf of all citizens.

The courts are like the referees of a sporting event. They stand between the government and the individual to ensure that both play by the rules of the game. If they fail to decide questions, the game can get out of control. The Constitution provides the basic rules. It is the duty of the courts to apply the Constitution to particular factual situations presented to them.

The U.S. Constitution and the constitutions of the various states contain provisions designed to limit the power of government over individuals. These provisions contain in broad language the fundamentals of freedom. These are accepted by all of us in their general and abstract form. There is probably near-universal agreement that we ought to have free speech, that a person accused of a crime ought to have an attorney, that the state should not inflict cruel and unusual punishments, and that people in similar circumstances ought to be treated equally by the government.

The courts, however, have the difficult task of applying these abstractions to specific cases. It is the courts that must decide what is a cruel and unusual punishment, when people are not being treated equally, or when a person is entitled to be represented by an attorney. These are difficult decisions. Courts can act only when an individual asks them to decide a controversy by filing a lawsuit. But when asked, the court cannot say, "That is too hard a question" or "I don't want to decide it now." And they must put the reasons for their decision in writing for all to examine.

The courts have recognized that sometimes the interest of the government is so great that the rights of the individual must be narrowed. Thus, even though the Constitution says that Congress shall make no law abridging the freedom of speech, the courts have indicated that falsely yelling "Fire!" in a crowded theater is unconstitutional. And laws against perjury are not prohibited by the First Amendment. The courts must balance the interest of the government and the interest of the individual. It is a difficult task. It is an imprecise task, but it must be done.

Enforcement of some of the rules may make it more difficult for one team or the other. Applying the rules of the Constitution to corrections temporarily may make it more difficult to retain control of offenders. But this country has aspirations and goals in addition to the control of those convicted of crime. Fairness, justice, and respect for individual dignity also must be given priority.

Many people ask, "How can courts change their mind and rule one way one day and one way the next?" The answer is that all law changes. The demands of the Constitution are both general and flexible. What is cruel and unusual punishment today might not have been so in earlier times. The interests of the government also change as times change. The courts have kept our Constitution up to date and can be expected to continue to do so.

Often, individuals ask, "How can one court in Indiana rule one way on the same day another court in Nebraska rules the opposite way?" They look at history, at other court decisions, at the mood and temper of the times, and at what rule seems reasonable. Two judges reasonably can come to different answers on such questions, the same as two correctional officers will differ as to the most effective way to deal with an inmate under their supervision.

Our judicial system is like a triangle, with the U.S. Supreme Court at the top. Thus, the Nebraska court can say what the law is, but its ruling affects only Nebraska. It is the same with the Indiana court. In the federal courts, an appeal can go to one of the twelve circuit courts whose rulings apply only to the states in that circuit. The Supreme Court rulings, of course, apply to everyone. Thus, until the Supreme Court decides an issue, there may be inconsistent rulings in the lower courts.

Courts began to be involved with correctional issues in the late 1960s. For a number of years after that, there often was controversy about the relationship of courts and corrections and about many specific issues. After more than twenty years of court oversight of corrections, much of this controversy has died away. An increasing number of fundamental principles have been established, reducing confusion among both correctional administrators and courts as to precisely what the rules of the game are. We now recognize that inmates have certain rights and that officers do also. Many courts have become more conservative in their approach to civil rights and are more apt to rule in favor of the institution than the inmate.

But some change in the law of corrections will continue simply because the law changes. While the change may not be as rapid as it was during the 1970s, disputes still will be presented by both inmates and staff to the courts for resolution, and some of the results in those cases will change the way correctional programs and facilities operate.

II.
A Short History of the Courts and Corrections

"I'll sue you!"

For someone entering the field of corrections in the last decade of the twentieth century, court involvement with correctional programs, inmate lawsuits (or threatened lawsuits), and the concept of "inmate rights" may seem like a sometimes annoying but still routine fact of life. But it has not always been this way. Many people working in corrections can remember when court involvement was simply unheard of, and wardens or jail administrators were the final arbiters of "inmate rights."

But since about 1970, litigation—or the threat of litigation—probably has had a greater effect on changing the way corrections does business than any other factor. It is hard to find any part of institutional operation that deals with inmates that has not been the subject of a lawsuit and court order.

And inmates are not the only ones filing lawsuits in corrections. Increasingly, employment-related issues are "legal issues." These range from employee discipline to discrimination to workplace safety.

The history of corrections and the courts can be divided into the following three eras:

1. The hands-off era, when courts simply would not respond to inmate claims. This period ran through most of the history of American corrections, but it began to wane around the middle to late 1960s.

2. The hands-on era, a time of rapidly increasing levels of court involvement with the operation of correctional institutions. This period ran from the demise of the hands-off period through most of the 1970s.

3. The one-hand-on, one-hand-off era saw a reduction of court intervention, caused by a series of decisions from the U.S. Supreme Court. These decisions generally embraced the idea that inmates are protected by the Constitution, but to a somewhat lesser degree than suggested by lower court decisions. This period ran through the 1980s and continues today.

The Hands-off Era

Typical of a court's approach to correctional issues during the hands-off era was that of an Alaska court that looked at conditions in a federal jail in Anchorage in 1951. The ancient wood frame jail housed up to forty inmates in a room that allowed less than nineteen square feet per inmate. Most of the floor space was consumed by bunks, tables, and benches. There were only twenty bunks for the forty inmates. There was no recreational capacity. Youths as young as sixteen were housed in the room. Health hazards existed due to the lack of ventilation, crowded conditions, and an inadequate number of toilets and showers (one each). Heat came from an old-fashioned coal-burning stove located in the room, which presented an obvious fire hazard. There was only a single exit, and an emergency exit could not have been added.

The judge said the room was not fit for human habitation and endorsed a description of the facility as a "fabulous obscenity." Although shocked by the conditions, the court refused to find an Eighth Amendment (cruel and unusual punishment) violation, noting that as bad as the conditions in the jail were, they were better than the conditions that soldiers fighting in the Korean War had to endure. The court also could find no relief that it could grant, short of simply releasing the inmates.*[1]

Many courts justified not getting involved with correctional cases on the basis that judges knew nothing about running a correctional facility; therefore, the court should defer almost totally to the decisions made by wardens or others responsible for running prisons or jails. Federal courts also were reluctant to get involved in issues of state or local government out of concerns over *federalism*, a concept that holds that federal courts, if at all possible, should avoid interfering in state or local government activities.

* *All footnotes are at the end of each chapter.*

During and before the 1960s, enormous discretion was left to correctional administrators about how their facilities were run. The court oversight that is common today did not exist. While state law set some outside limits, relatively little control was imposed on the day-to-day operation of a prison or jail. Even within a department of corrections, typically there was little centralized control. In many cases, "the law" within an institution was set—and enforced—by the warden or by individual officers in the cellblock.

Case Study: The "Courts Shouldn't Meddle" Defense

In 1966, a group of black inmates filed suit in federal court in Alabama attacking state laws that required racial segregation in state and local correctional facilities. In an era when similar equal protection challenges to racial segregation in all types of government activities filled the courts, the defendants' only response to the suit was to argue that racial segregation in prisons or jails was a "matter of routine prison security and discipline and (therefore was) not within the scope of permissible inquiry by the courts." The court rejected this defense, found the practices unconstitutional, and ordered the facilities desegregated. *Washington v. Lee*, 263 F.Supp. 327 (M.D. Ala., 1966), aff'd. 88 S.Ct. 994 (1968).

As long as the lid was kept on a prison, the public seemed to care little about what went on in the facility. A riot or scandal might call attention to a prison from time to time, but generally there was no active, regular review of prison practices or conditions.

The lack of public attention contributed to the physical and operational deterioration of many facilities. Funds to maintain or remodel old, worn-out institutions were hard to obtain since funding sources such as legislatures or county commissions saw little political reason to pour tax money into prison improvements.

This same political reality tended to keep operational appropriations low, so staff salaries stayed low, and little if any money was available for training. Correctional officers now often must attend and pass literally hundreds of hours of training in specialized academies before

7

being fully qualified to work. By comparison, a survey taken in the mid-1960s showed more than 40 percent of the state correctional systems did not even require a high school diploma for starting correctional officers.[2] Wardens often were appointed based on politics, not professionalism or experience.

This lack of almost any regular external oversight, combined with poorly trained staff and a lack of professional leadership, allowed serious abuses to develop in many facilities across the country. Examples of these abuses began to be presented to the courts in lawsuits.

During the 1950s and 1960s, courts, particularly federal courts, increasingly were involved in large reform lawsuits, beginning with the school desegregation cases. The 1960s was an era of civil rights attention and reform. Public attention focused on many groups outside the mainstream of American culture, and efforts were made to improve the lives of those groups.

With this heightened concern for civil rights in general, it was inevitable that conditions and practices in correctional facilities would receive attention. And unfortunately, those facilities and their management often were totally unprepared for such scrutiny. Frequently, the practices or conditions that were the subject of suits really could not be defended as being appropriate under any theory of modern penology. Administrators and their lawyers often reacted to potential court intervention by ignoring the facts of the case or the legal theories under which the case was brought and instead argued that the court had no business "meddling" in the operation of the prison or jail. This sort of emotional response was increasingly unsuccessful.

The End of the Hands-off Era

What led to the end of the hands-off era? It was a combination of factors. Civil rights issues were coming to the courts from many directions. The mood of the country favored reform and improving conditions for the less fortunate, and many young lawyers were interested in working with reform cases. But more than anything else, the facts of the cases that got to court were what led to the end of the hands-off period.

1. As late as 1965, whipping was allowed in the Arkansas prison system. The decision to whip an inmate was left to the person

who would do the whipping. Supposedly, a limitation of ten lashes per offense was imposed. In some cases, inmate-trusties were allowed to whip other inmates. Whippings were administered on the bare buttocks of the inmates. In the same system, the infamous "Tucker telephone" was used to administer electric shocks to inmates as a form of punishment. These sorts of punishments were given without any form of a hearing to determine if the inmate, in fact, had violated a rule.[3]

2. The first overall prison conditions case also came from Arkansas. Armed inmates (trusties) guarded other inmates. Only two correctional officers were on duty at night in a prison holding nearly 1,000 men. Abuses of the trusty system—bribery, extortion, smuggling, and so forth—were common.

Most inmates in the Arkansas prisons were housed in dormitories. Placement in a particular unit was based on race (blacks were segregated) and rank in the institution. No free-world staff entered the dorms at night. Inmate "floor walkers" were responsible for keeping order, but were ineffective. It was common for inmates to creep from one bunk to another to stab an enemy. Rape was common, and at night, the floor walkers would not interfere with a sexual assault.

The trusties also commonly interfered with access to medical services. Sanitation in the kitchen was described as "deplorable." The judge who reviewed overall conditions in this system called it "a dark and evil world completely alien to the free world, a world that is administered by criminals under unwritten codes and customs completely foreign to free-world culture."[4]

3. In Alabama, a suit was filed dealing with medical care. Inmates there routinely handled both treatment and records. In one situation, a maggot-infested wound went twenty days before anything was done to change the dressings or clean and disinfect it. An incontinent patient was kept sitting on a bench so he wouldn't soil the bedclothes. His condition caused him to fall a lot. Eventually, his leg had to be amputated. Sanitation in the medical department was poor. There was a serious shortage of qualified doctors.[5]

4. In another case, death row inmates were locked in their six-by-nine cells all but fifteen minutes a day. This regimen lasted as long as the inmate remained on death row, up to nine years in

9

one situation. This led the court to order out-of-the-cell exercise and led to later cases requiring outdoor exercise several times a week.[6]

Case Study: Rehabilitation Programs: Not a Right, But. . .

Courts consistently agreed with the general principle that there was no constitutional right to rehabilitation or rehabilitation programs for inmates. But sometimes courts would order such programs to be developed anyway.

One court reasoned that inmates had a right not to be housed in a setting that was actually counterproductive to rehabilitation, in other words, conditions that cause degeneration. Where the New Hampshire State Prison conditions involved pervasive idleness, only make-work jobs, and very few meaningful vocational or educational programs, the court felt it was creating unconstitutional degenerative conditions that were counterproductive to rehabilitation.

Given those conclusions, the court then ordered the institution to provide each inmate with the opportunity to participate in educational and recreational programs and to learn a skill marketable in New Hampshire. *Laaman v. Helgemoe*, 437 F.Supp. 269 (D.N.H., 1977).

The courts that heard these early cases were reluctant to abandon the hands-off approach, but were clearly shocked by the facts presented by the inmates and their lawyers. The defendants—the people accountable for running the facilities—offered little or no responsible justification for their actions other than perhaps to plead a lack of funding. But it was clear that unless the courts intervened in some way, the shocking, violent, and inhumane practices would continue. Faced with the choice of allowing the conditions and practices to continue or intervening to try to prevent them from continuing, courts began to intervene, and the hands-off era became history.

The Hands-on Era

The hands-on era began with courts responding to the sorts of shocking situations described. Many cases dealt with conditions, but others dealt with operational issues such as due process in disciplinary hearings and under what circumstances inmate religious freedoms could be restricted.

The courts' sudden involvement with correctional issues created a great deal of controversy among correctional administrators, some of which continues to the present. The controversy was compounded because of several factors. Courts never had looked over corrections' shoulder before. Because correctional law as a separate area of legal concern was invented around 1970, there were no court *precedents* (earlier cases establishing fundamental principles in correctional law) to guide the courts or prepare institutional administrators or their lawyers to defend their positions. A number of lawyers around the country aggressively began litigating on behalf of inmates, trying to use the courts almost as super legislative bodies to create and enforce new correctional policy in all sorts of areas.

Given the lack of precedent, new rights were created and grew rapidly. An example is the right to exercise. Probably the first case where exercise was an issue involved the extreme situation of death row inmates mentioned earlier. They lived for years in six-by-nine foot cells with little natural light and were allowed out of their cells for only fifteen minutes per day. The court found these conditions to be cruel and unusual punishment and ordered the inmates be provided outdoor exercise.[7] There was no real discussion of the effect of the lack of exercise on inmates nor consideration of whether indoor exercise could have met the inmates' needs.

Soon the "right" that had been created for death row inmates locked in their cells twenty-three hours and forty-five minutes per day was found to apply to jail inmates.[8] Then, another court was talking about the "fundamental" right to exercise and the importance of inmates being able to see the open sky, sun, and clouds.[9]

So, in a matter of only a few years, courts had gone from never having talked about inmate exercise rights, to finding a need for exercise in a very extreme situation, to deciding exercise was a fundamental right somehow related to being able to see the sun and perhaps feel the wind in one's face. The confusion that was created by this sort of approach is reflected in the variation in the amount of exercise courts required. Some said an hour per day every day. Others said an hour per day for three-to-five days per week was sufficient. Most courts came to recognize that a few days without exercise would not violate a right. Still others were less concerned about the outdoor aspect than being sure the exercise space was large enough (and perhaps equipped) for large muscle exercise. It was obvious that year-round outdoor exercise was not possible in much of the country where weather conditions would not permit it.

The sort of confusion that the exercise issue typifies was resolved somewhat by the Supreme Court's two major conditions of confinement decisions in which the Court said the key question about the adequacy of conditions was the effect they had on inmates.[10] Now, a condition or practice (such as the lack of exercise) must be shown to have a serious effect on inmates before it may be unconstitutional.

Other examples of the extent of court involvement during the decade of the 1970s include the following:

1. One court ordered that the prison daily diet must include "at least one fresh green vegetable, one fresh yellow vegetable, and serving of meat or protein-provided meat substitute." This requirement was reversed on appeal.[11]
2. A decision involving many conditions and practices at a new federal jail in New York City was more than fifty pages long. The district court required officials to allow pretrial detainees (but not convicted inmates) to be present during cell searches. Double-celling (placing two inmates in a cell designed for one) was found unconstitutional. Pretrial detainees were allowed to wear their own clothing or uniforms, but jail jumpsuits were not permitted by the court.[12]

Probably the most significant trends among lower courts during the 1970s were the assumption that double-celling was automatically unconstitutional and the increased reliance on professional standards (such as those set by the American Correctional Association). Despite the controversy created by the sudden and dramatic involvement of the courts in corrections, one must wonder, in hindsight, if many of the admittedly very serious problems the courts addressed would have been addressed and corrected in any other way had the courts maintained their hands-off approach.

The One-hand-on, One-hand-off Era

The momentum lower courts built up in corrections cases during the 1970s began to slow as the decade approached its conclusion. The main reason for this slowing was the U.S. Supreme Court. It takes years for a case to get from a federal district court, through the court of appeals, to the Supreme Court. While the Supreme Court is asked to review many cases, it selects only a few for consideration—cases that the Court believes raise especially important legal issues. Since the concepts of correctional law and inmate rights barely had begun to develop in 1970, it is then not surprising that few cases or issues got to the Supreme Court before the late 1970s.

As correctional issues slowly found their way to the Court, another development was taking place: many of the liberal justices who made up the "Warren Court" of the 1950s and 1960s were retiring and were replaced by more conservative justices. So, by the second half of the 1970s, a somewhat conservative Court awaited the correctional law cases that were coming to the Court for decision.

One of the first suggestions of the Court's conservatism came in a case in which the issue was whether a prison rule prohibiting an inmates' "labor union" violated the inmates' First Amendment rights of free speech and association.[13] The Court upheld the ban. Perhaps more significant than the immediate result was what the Court said about courts deferring to the judgment and concerns of prison officials: "It is enough to say that they have not been conclusively shown to be wrong in this view" (that an inmates' labor union would be a threat to security and order in the prison). What the Court was saying was that the officials did not have to prove their concerns. Instead, those attacking the concerns had to prove they were wrong or exaggerated.

But the most dramatic indication of the direction the Court wanted to go with correctional issues came in the case of *Bell v. Wolfish*,[14] probably the single most important corrections case the court ever has decided. *Bell* was a major crowding/conditions of confinement case that involved a new federal jail in Manhattan. The district court had found many conditions and practices in the facility unconstitutional. Some, but not all, of the district court's order was appealed to the court

13

of appeals, which upheld some portions and reversed others. Some of the issues from the court of appeals' decision then were taken to the Supreme Court. Though the case that got to the Supreme Court was much narrower than the case decided by the district court, it still contained some very important issues, the most significant of which was the question of whether double-celling inmates violated the Constitution.

The Court specifically rejected the idea that single-celling was constitutionally required. The Court said there was "no one-man, one-cell principle lurking" in the Constitution and approved double-bunking in the jail under review.[15] The Court said that factors such as the time out of the cell and the activities available to inmates were more important considerations than just the number of inmates in a cell. The Court also rejected correctional standards (such as American Correctional Association standards) as a measure of the Constitution.

The Court refused to hold that the presumption of innocence enjoyed by pretrial detainees somehow was relevant to judging the conditions of confinement in a jail. Lower courts were criticized for becoming "enmeshed in the minutiae of prison operations." The case also approved rules that allow inmates to receive books or publications only from the publishers (publishers-only rules) and a policy of strip searching inmates after returning from contact visits.

Bell then began to send a message to lower courts that while inmates did enjoy constitutional rights, those rights were more subject to restriction than many courts had suggested. The "slow down" message of the Supreme Court was repeated in several due process cases. The Court ruled that transfers into administrative segregation were not inherently protected by the Fourteenth Amendment.[16] Nor did due process protect an inmate who was transferred from one prison to another, even if the transfer was over thousands of miles.[17] The latter half of the 1980s saw the Court state even more clearly that lower courts should defer to the judgment and concerns of prison officials. In a series of cases, the Court set out a specific test for courts to evaluate cases that involved a conflict between an inmate's constitutionally protected interests and a legitimate interest of the institution. This test makes restrictions on inmates' constitutional rights easier to defend than was the case under the approaches most lower courts had taken previously.

During the same years that the Supreme Court was telling lower courts to slow down and not substitute their judgment about how best to run a prison for the judgment of the persons hired and trained to do this difficult job, the level of professionalism in institutions was growing. Line staff were better trained and supervised.

Carefully developed policies and procedures replaced "the seat of the pants" as a guide for making decisions. An increasing number of agencies worked to be formally accredited. Many states adopted jail standards and inspected jails for compliance with those standards. Institutions began to follow the now well-developed case law that existed for many areas of prison and jail operations. Thus, institutions were able to defend themselves better than they had in the early years of the inmate rights movement.

Congress and Inmate Lawsuits:
The Prison Litigation Reform Act (PLRA)

Perhaps the most significant single development in correctional law during the decade of the 1990s did not come from the courts defining a new inmate right or modifying an old one. The development came from the U.S. Congress in the form of the Prison Litigation Reform Act (PLRA).

Many have criticized the entire inmate rights movement for resulting in inmates filing thousands upon thousands of lawsuits every year. Most of the cases are filed in federal district court and most are dismissed prior to trial in favor of defendants. Other criticism has been directed at federal courts for taking an overly active role in controlling or directing actions of correctional agencies, and for becoming too "enmeshed in the minutiae of prison operations."[18]

The numbers of inmate cases certainly speak for themselves. In 1970, in the earliest days of the inmate rights movement, state and federal inmates filed less than 2,200 civil rights complaints.[19] In 1995, the number topped 40,000, nearly a twenty-fold increase.[20] While this is obviously a huge increase, it is tempered when one takes into account the increase in the number of inmates. Between 1980 and 1995, the number of inmates in federal and state prisons increased from approximately 320,000 to 1.1 million. The rate at which prisoners filed federal court petitions of all sorts per 1,000 inmates (mainly civil rights and habeas corpus petitions) actually declined by 17 percent between 1980

15

and 1996.[21] The rate of lawsuits per 1,000 inmates aside, 40,000 civil rights petitions from inmates is still a large number of lawsuits.

And what of the merit of those 40,000 civil rights cases? Less than 3 percent of the civil rights cases inmates filed in federal court in 1995 actually went to trial. In only about 1 percent was a judgment entered which was wholly or partially in the inmate's favor, not a very good success rate.[22]

In the PLRA, Congress responded to criticisms of inmates filing too many meritless cases and of courts micromanaging prisons by passing a package of laws, which makes it more difficult for inmates to file cases, somewhat easier for courts to dismiss cases, and which limits the power of the federal courts to enter relief against a prison after the court finds constitutional violations. The PLRA also makes it easier for correctional officials to terminate court orders that have been entered against them.

The details of the PLRA will be discussed elsewhere in this book. However, in general terms, the PLRA makes it harder for inmates to file lawsuits in several ways. The most significant is that the law requires inmates to pay a full filing fee (through what amounts to a down payment and subsequent "EZ monthly payments") even though they may be indigent. Previously, a court could waive the filing fee altogether. Additionally, PLRA creates a sort of "three strikes and you're out" provision. That section of the law says any inmate who has had three cases dismissed as frivolous, malicious, or which "fail to state a claim for which relief can be granted" is barred from filing any new cases without paying the full filing fee when the case is filed, unless the inmate alleges he is under "imminent danger of serious physical harm."[23] PLRA also requires that inmates exhaust all administrative remedies (such as grievances and internal appeals) before filing a civil rights case. It also reduces the size of attorneys' fees which can be awarded.

The law demands that any relief a court orders be narrowly drawn and go no further than necessary to correct whatever violation the court has found.[24] The law makes it more difficult for courts to enter prisoner release orders.[25] Probably the most significant limitation on the court's powers is the section of the law which makes it easier for defendants to successfully demand that old court orders be terminated.[26] Over the last thirty years, it has not been uncommon for major prison or jail reform cases to last ten or twenty years, with sometimes bitter litigation

16

continuing over the question of whether government officials had complied with sometimes very detailed requirements mandated by a court or agreed to by defendants in a consent decree. The Prison Litigation Reform Act makes it much easier for defendants to terminate such long running cases, effectively creating a requirement that two years after an order has been entered in a reform case, if the defendants ask that the order be terminated, the plaintiffs must prove that constitutional violations continue in order for the court to be able to retain jurisdiction. Ironically, it is not uncommon for defendants to choose not to ask for old orders to be terminated where, for instance, an order imposes a population cap on an institution, which is the only thing preventing the institution from becoming very crowded.

One impact of the PLRA, which stands out, demonstrates that the law is meeting at least one of the goals of its sponsors. In 1995, the year before the PLRA was passed, state inmates filed more than 40,500 civil rights cases in federal court. In 1998, that number had dropped to around 25,400.[27] When one considers that the number of civil rights cases filed by state inmates had increased every year except one since 1970 (1990 filings dropped nearly 200 from 1989, but bounced back the next year), a drop of 15,000 cases is unprecedented.

While the major aspects of the Prison Litigation Reform Act have been challenged as unconstitutional, courts generally have upheld all of the major aspects of the Act.

The Future of Court Intervention and Corrections

The era of expanding inmate rights is clearly over, replaced by a time of reduced court intervention in corrections. Almost every Supreme Court decision since the 1980s has trimmed back what lower courts have said about the rights of inmates. In some cases, the Supreme Court even has retreated from what it had said in earlier decisions.

For example, in 1974, the Court at least appeared to say that inmates were entitled to due process protections when facing disciplinary charges for which they could be put in segregation (notice, a hearing, a limited right to call witnesses, and so forth).[28] Twenty-one years later, in 1995, the Court held no due process protections existed for an inmate facing a disciplinary sanction of thirty days in segregation.[29] In addition to "reinterpreting" what it said in 1974, the Court in the

Sandin case also completely rejected its own interpretation of how lower courts should decide if due process protections applied to almost any decision a prison or jail might make which adversely affected an inmate.[30]

In 1996, the Court revisited a 1977 decision regarding access to the courts in a case called *Lewis v. Casey*.[31] *Lewis* upheld the basic principles from the earlier case, that inmates have a constitutionally protected right of access to the courts and that prison officials have a duty to assist inmates in the preparation and filing of meaningful legal papers. At the same time, the court in *Lewis* reinterpreted how these principles should be applied. The result: it is considerably harder for an inmate to win an access to the courts case, especially if the inmate is claiming that law library resources were insufficient.

As noted in the previous section, the decision by Congress to pass the Prison Litigation Reform Act sets up barriers. The inmates must surmount them to get a case to court. Congress also attempted to put checks on the power of federal courts to oversee facilities found to be unconstitutional in some way.

Despite pressure for reduced court involvement with corrections, court oversight over many practices and conditions in jails and prisons will continue, and persons working in corrections, from the newest officer to the longtime warden, need to remain sensitive to the rights of inmates. Conditions of confinement will continue to be a major concern, for no other reason than the fact that jail and prison populations continue to climb. This unfortunately assures that many facilities will remain seriously crowded. While crowding is not necessarily unconstitutional, serious constitutional problems often are the product of crowding, as a soaring inmate population outstrips the ability of an institution to provide for the basic human needs of the inmates.

In many respects, courts in the future will be called upon to enforce existing rights, such as in the areas of medical care and use of force. However, some new issues will continue to emerge. Problems often have arisen in recent years concerning sexual contact between staff and inmates. This is an unfortunate by-product of the growth of cross-gender work forces. The numbers of elderly inmates in prison will continue to grow substantially over the next ten years as prison terms get longer and—if some prognosticators are correct—more crimes are committed by the elderly.

Another possible development, already visible in some states, is that state courts will become more active in inmate cases. Where the federal courts are retreating from protection of inmate rights, litigators will reexamine state courts as a possible source of relief. State laws or constitutions can require more than does the federal Constitution. More and more state courts will be tested for their receptivity to inmate rights issues.

Another development of recent years is the increased willingness of staff to assert their legal rights through lawsuits against government agencies. Congress expanded the legal rights of persons with disabilities when it passed the Americans With Disabilities Act of 1990 (ADA). This sweeping law and its accompanying federal regulations provide protections for employees (and job applicants), inmates, and even for persons visiting correctional institutions. The ADA undoubtedly will be the source of numerous lawsuits affecting corrections as the twentieth century winds to a close.

While a reduction of court oversight is welcomed by many, it brings with it the seeds of potential problems later. The threat of lawsuits over the last twenty years contributed to correctional professionals becoming much more sensitive about understanding what legally they can and cannot do. If the threat of litigation subsides in many areas, the incentive to obey the law created by that threat may erode. And if this occurs, serious abuses may increase. In a worst-case scenario, a few such gross abuses could come to the attention of the courts and trigger a resurrection of the hands-on era, with courts again seeing themselves as the only protection available to inmates.

To a large degree, whether this worst-case scenario comes to pass will depend on the professionalism of the men and women working in corrections. If they insist on doing their jobs in accordance with recognized professional standards and practices, there will be little reason for court involvement. But if such benchmarks are abandoned, and facilities and individual staff are left to drift with little supervision or training, serious problems are likely to emerge and bring a new era of court intervention.

Review Questions

1. What were the three periods or eras of court involvement with corrections?

2. List two factors that led to the courts first becoming involved with correctional issues.

3. In passing the Prison Litigation Reform Act, Congress attempted to realize what two major goals?

4. Is the Supreme Court requiring lower courts to show increased or decreased deference to the judgment of correctional officers and administrators?

Notes

1. *Ex Parte Pickens*, 101 F.Supp. 285 (D. Alas., 1951).
2. *Task Force Report: Corrections*, p. 181, President's Commission on Law Enforcement and Administration of Justice, 1967.
3 *Jackson v. Bishop*, 404 F.2d 571 (8th Cir., 1968).
4. *Holt v. Sarver*, 309 F.Supp. 362 (E.D. Ark., 1970).
5. *Newman v. Alabama*, 503 F.2d 1320 (5th Cir., 1974).
6. *Sinclair v. Henderson*, 331 F.Supp. 1123 (D. La., 1971).
7. *Sinclair v. Henderson*.
8. *Taylor v. Sterret*, 334 F.Supp. 411 (N.D. Tex., 1972).
9. *Rhem v. Malcolm*, 371 F.Supp. 594 (S.D.N.Y., 1974); 432 F.Supp. at 782.
10. *Bell v. Wolfish*, 441 U.S. 529 (1979). *Rhodes v. Chapman*, 452 U.S. 337 (1981).
11. *Smith v. Sullivan*, 563 F.2d 373 (5th Cir., 1977).
12. U.S. *ex rel. Wolfish v. Levy,* 439 F.Supp. 114 (S.D.N.Y., 1977). Portions of this decision were later reversed in *Bell v. Wolfish*.
13. *Jones v. North Carolina Prisoners' Labor Union*, 433 U.S. 119 (1977).
14. 441 U.S. 529 (1979).
15. 441 U.S. at 542.

16. *Hewitt v. Helms*, 103 S.Ct. 864 (1982).

17. *Olim v. Wakinekona*, 461 U.S. 238 (1983).

18. *Bell v. Wolfish*, 441 U.S. 520, 562 (1979).

19. *Sourcebook of Criminal Justice Statistics*,1983, p. 514. U.S. Department of Justice, Bureau of Justice Statistics.

20. *Prisoner Petitions in the Federal Courts,* 1980 – 96, Table 2, p. 3. Bureau of Justice Statistics, 1997; hereafter, "Prisoner Petitions."

21. *Prisoner Petitions*, p. 5.

22. Id., p. 6.

23. 28 USC §1915(g).

24. 18 USC § 3626(a)

25. Id.

26. Id.

27. *Sourcebook of Criminal Justice Statistics*, 1999, p. 442. Department of Justice, Bureau of Justice Statistics.

28. *Wolff v. McDonnell*, 4180 U.S. 539 (1974).

29. *Sandin v. Conner*, 115 S.Ct. 2293 (1995).

30. *See Hewitt v. Helms*, 459 U.S. 460 (1983).

31. 518 U.S. 343 (1996), *Bounds v. Smith*, 430 U.S. 817 (1977).

III.
Types of Lawsuits Inmates File

Almost all litigation filed by inmates falls into one of three categories: (1) civil rights actions, in which the inmate claims a condition or practice of the institution violates a constitutional right of the inmate, (2) habeas corpus actions, in which the inmate challenges the legality of being in custody at all, and (3) tort suits, in which the inmate claims he or she was damaged as the result of the negligence of someone.

The Civil Rights Act

The overwhelming majority of lawsuits filed by offenders that involve correctional personnel are civil rights actions brought under a federal statute, 42 United States Code Section 1983, commonly known as the Civil Rights Act. The Civil Rights Act was passed by Congress in 1871 and reads as follows:

> Every person who, under color of any statute, ordinance, regulation, custom, or usage, of any state or territory, subjects, or causes to be subject, any citizen of the United States or other person within the jurisdiction thereof to the deprivation of any rights, privileges, or immunities secured by the Constitution and laws, shall be liable to the party injured in an action at law, suit in equity, or other proper proceeding for redress.

The act was originally passed to address wrongs done by the Ku Klux Klan in the post-Civil War South. For decades the law received little usage. It was "rediscovered" by the civil rights movement in the 1950s and 1960s and became the major vehicle for much of the civil rights litigation of that era. Subsequently, "Section 1983," as the act often is referred to, became commonly used in all forms of civil rights litigation, including the prisoners' rights movement that began in the late 1960s.

Civil rights suits typically are filed in federal district court. However, they also can be filed in state court.

To have a legitimate claim under Section 1983 (in legal jargon "to state a claim"), the plaintiff must establish that a person, acting under color of state law, caused a violation of constitutional rights or federal statutory rights. On establishing such a violation, the violator can be found liable for either damages or for other forms of judicially ordered relief.

Defendants must be "persons"

Civil rights actions only can be brought against persons and cannot be brought directly against the state (or state agencies), since the state and its agencies are not considered persons. Interestingly, the Supreme Court has ruled that municipal corporations (cities, counties, and so forth) are persons and can be sued directly in a civil rights action.[1] The "person" issue becomes important with regard to damages in Section 1983 suits. Since the state is not a person, the state cannot be sued directly for damages under Section 1983. But units of local government can be and often are sued for damages since they are now persons under Section 1983.

Color of state law

As a general rule, the suits can be brought only against government employees for actions arising out of their employment, in other words, employees acting "under color of state law." Thus, a civil rights action cannot be brought against an offender since the actions of the offender are not taken under color of state law. In a case brought by an inmate against a private doctor who worked for the prison under a contract, the Supreme Court held that the doctor was still considered to be acting under color of state law and thus subject to possible liability under Section 1983.[2] This case stands for the principle that employees of private prison companies are subject to suit under Section 1983.

> # Case Study: Section 1983 and a Federal Statutory Right
>
> One area where Section 1983 may become an important tool for enforcing federal statutes in corrections is with regard to the practice of holding juveniles in adult jails. This practice, which is uniformly frowned on by correctional administrators, occurs far less than it used to, but it still does occur.
>
> A federal law, part of the Juvenile Justice and Delinquency Prevention Act, provides that jurisdictions that accept federal money under the act may not continue to house juveniles in adult jails. The question has come up as to whether a juvenile who is housed in an adult jail may sue for a violation of the act, or whether only the federal government may bring such a suit. Some courts have said that juveniles do have such a right and that their claims may be brought under Section 1983. *Doe v. Borough of Clifton Heights*, 719 F.Supp. 382.(E. D. Pa., 1989).

Must prove violation of Constitution or federal statute

The action must establish a violation of a constitutional right (generally a right guaranteed by the Bill of Rights and/or the Fourteenth Amendment to the U.S. Constitution) or a violation of a federal statutory right. Violation of federal statutes rarely are alleged in correctional litigation because very few federal statutes protect inmates.

Personal involvement

The general rule is that to be liable, a defendant actually must have participated in, in other words, caused, the constitutional violation. Liability may not be imposed simply because the defendant has some supervisory authority over the individual whose direct actions caused the violation. Under a legal doctrine known as respondeat superior, automatic liability can be imposed in tort actions (discussed later in this chapter) against an employer based on acts by an employee, but not in civil rights actions. In other words, in a 1983 action, the defendant must cause the injury to the plaintiff.

> # Case Study: Tolerating Violence Leads to Supervisory Liability
>
> The arrestee, who had attempted to shoot a police officer, was brought to the holding facility and beaten by several officers, even though supervisors were present during the beating. The inmate again was beaten that night, and the night supervisor did nothing to prevent it, although evidence showed he knew it was going to happen.
>
> The sheriff, not present for any of the beatings, was found liable for damages of $125,000. This liability was based in part on the fact that supervisors knew of the beatings and did nothing to prevent them. The court felt the sheriff helped conceal the incidents by failing to investigate them. The failure to investigate also suggested to the court that the sheriff "ratified" the illegal beatings. *Marchese v. Lucas*, 758 F.2d 1816 (6th Cir., 1985).

Supervisory liability

Section 1983 imposes liability when someone "causes one to be subject to" a constitutional violation. Courts may be asked to focus on this language to assess potential liability on supervisory personnel who did not directly participate in the challenged act or omission. Such cases often focus on one of two specific areas:

1. **Failure to Supervise**. Where a supervisory staff member has (or reasonably should have) knowledge of a pattern of constitutionally offensive acts but fails to take remedial steps, liability may attach if the supervisor's actions or inactions can be said to be "deliberately indifferent" to the constitutional rights of the victim. An example of this might be where a supervisor is aware of and apparently condones staff using excessive force against inmates.

2. **Failure to Train**. If a failure to train is so serious as to reflect "deliberate indifference" to the constitutional rights of someone, the agency (but rarely, if ever, the supervisor) may be held liable.[3] This might occur if a supervisor assigned a new staff member to a constitutionally sensitive position knowing the

person assigned did not have training in the constitutional issues involved.

For instance, suppose a correctional officer was assigned to a prison law library without understanding that inmates may have a constitutionally protected right to use the library as part of their right of access to the courts. Refusal to allow an inmate to use the library because the officer felt the inmate was "wasting too much time in the library" could expose the supervisor to liability even though the supervisor was not directly involved in the actions of the officer.

There are other supervisory failures that potentially can lead to supervisory liability. These include such things as improper supervision or assignment, gross failures in hiring and retention (hiring and/or retaining clearly incompetent staff), failures in direction of staff, and so forth.

The common link in all of these areas is where the supervisor's alleged failure can be tied directly to the actual violation, and it can be said that but for the failure of the supervisor, this violation probably would not have occurred. In this sense, the courts will say that the supervisor "caused" the violation.

Most lawsuits about improper training or supervision are not brought against the trainer or first-level supervisor. Instead, the agency or agency head is sued, the lawsuit claims that the inadequate training or supervision reflected agency policy or custom

Forms of Relief under the Civil Rights Act

Two basic forms of relief are available under the Civil Rights Act for the plaintiff who establishes that his or her rights have been violated.

Injunctions

Injunctions are orders from a court to a defendant that require the defendant to stop (or start) doing something. For example, "Stop denying inmates their proper right of access to the courts," or "To meet your obligations to provide inmates with meaningful access to the courts, provide a properly equipped law library."

Injunctions are historically the most common form of relief under the Civil Rights Act and are what frequently led to the (generally inappropriate) complaint that courts are improperly meddling with state affairs. Injunctions under Section 1983 have led to the reshaping and reformatting of entire correctional systems.

Failure to comply with an injunction subjects the defendant to potential sanctions for contempt of court, including fines and even imprisonment. Failure to comply with injunctions worded in general terms also frequently has led to more specific injunctions, particularly in conditions of confinement suits.

The Prison Litigation Reform Act (PLRA) attempts to reduce the power of the federal courts to enter injunctions in jail and prison cases. First, any injunction must be "narrowly drawn, extend no further than necessary to correct the violation of the federal right, and [be] the least intrusive means necessary to correct the violation of the Federal right."[4]

The PLRA also forbids courts from issuing orders that have the effect of reducing or limiting a prison population, such as a population cap or release orders, until other less intrusive forms of relief have been attempted for a reasonable period of time and found to be inadequate[5] Even then, only a three-judge court can enter a prisoner release order.

Within a few months of the PLRA's passage, the Supreme Court also discussed the power of lower courts to order injunctive relief against prison officials. In *Lewis v. Casey*,[6] the Court was quite critical of a very detailed relief order a district court entered in an access to the courts case (*see* Chapter IV for a discussion of this aspect of the decision). *Lewis* emphasizes that when a lower court finds constitutional violations in a correctional facility, it should consider the view of prison officials in formulating a relief order and try to defer to the judgment of those officials. A court should try to avoid becoming too involved in overseeing day-to-day operational matters. The general tone of the *Lewis* decision is very similar to that of the PLRA, although interestingly, the *Lewis* opinion does not mention the PLRA.

Damages

Monetary damages are available under Section 1983. Damages are of the following three types:

1. **Nominal**. Where the plaintiff's rights were violated but the plaintiff can show no actual harm, the plaintiff is entitled only to "nominal" damages, usually $1.00.

2. **Compensatory**. These compensate the plaintiff for injuries actually suffered. They include such objective factors as lost wages and medical expenses. Compensatory damages also are available for more subjective forms of loss such as pain and suffering and mental anguish.
3. **Punitive**. Punitive damages are intended to punish the wrongdoer and deter similar sorts of conduct by others in the future. They usually are awarded only when the defendant knowingly violated the Constitution and/or acted in reckless disregard of the rights of the plaintiff.

Where the right allegedly violated was not "clearly established," the defendant will be granted a "qualified immunity" and cannot be required to pay damages. This is sometimes known as the "good faith" defense. It is court-created and recognizes that government officials should not be held liable in damages for failing to accurately predict the future course of constitutional law. It protects only employees—it does not protect a government agency if that agency, such as a city or county, is otherwise subject to damages. The good faith defense only protects against damages, not against injunctive relief.

Despite the implications of the name "good faith defense," an employee's subjective good intentions or good faith are of little relevance in establishing a good faith defense. Rather than focusing on the employee's state of mind, the good faith defense focuses almost entirely on the state of the law at the time of the incident: whether the law was "clearly established" is the key question.

Employees of private corrections companies do not have any qualified immunity protection. In 1997, the Supreme Court said that the policy reasons that underlay protecting governmental employees from damages liability unless a constitutional right was clearly established do not extend to employees of private companies, even though they are doing the same work as correctional officials employed by government agencies.[7]

In some situations, even broader immunity is available, as in the case where a probation officer is acting so closely with a sentencing judge that a court will afford the probation officer complete judicial or quasi-judicial immunity. Judicial or quasi-judicial immunity affords the person protected by it almost complete immunity from damage lawsuits. In general, only qualified (not quasi-judicial) immunity is available for most correctional employees.

In 1986, the Supreme Court decided if hearing officers in prison disciplinary hearings were entitled to quasi-judicial immunity. These officials make a great many constitutionally important decisions, and they decide disciplinary cases, which is somewhat comparable to what judges do. But the Court refused to extend complete immunity to these officials, at least as long as they are still direct subordinates of the warden and are subject to pressure from other correctional staff to decide cases in favor of the institution.[8]

As correctional law continues to evolve and develop, an increasing number of rights are becoming "clearly established." Therefore, potential damage liability is increasing.

Attorneys' fees

Under another part of the United States Code, 42 USC 1988, the prevailing party in a civil rights action is entitled to be awarded attorneys' fees. The Attorneys' Fees Act primarily benefits prevailing plaintiffs since the law has been interpreted to allow fees for prevailing defendants only when the plaintiff's action can be shown to have been frivolous (a difficult burden to meet).

Prior to passage of the Prison Litigation Reform Act, courts generally interpreted the Attorneys' Fee Act liberally under the theory that by encouraging civil rights litigation, more civil rights violations would be brought to the attention of the courts and corrected, thus furthering the underlying purposes of the Civil Rights Act. The general method of computing fees was to multiply the hours the lawyer spent on the case times the lawyer's hourly billing rate. This produced a so-called "lodestar" figure, which might be adjusted up or down slightly. Fee awards based on hourly rates over $200—sometimes over $300—per hour were not uncommon. Courts sometimes gave fee awards worth many times more than the judgment, which the plaintiff won. Very large, complex cases could generate fees in the millions of dollars.

The PLRA changes this. The law places a cap on the hourly rate that must be paid at probably around $120 per hour or less in most jurisdictions. Fees must bear a reasonable relationship to the size of the judgment awarded the plaintiff. These and other restrictions should reduce the size of attorneys' fee awards considerably. However, even with these limitations, attorneys' fees will remain an important part of inmate civil rights litigation.

While it sounds like the possibility of obtaining a fee award in excess of $200 per hour would have attracted many lawyers in private practice to the field of correctional law, in fact this does not appear to have been the case. However, to the extent that lawyers were attracted by the possibility of obtaining such fees (after perhaps years of litigating a case without receiving any money), reducing the possible fee award to $120 per hour or less is likely to discourage private lawyers from representing inmates.

Grievances

Most prisons and jails have had some form of inmate grievance system in place for many years. Under a law known as the Civil Rights of Institutionalized Persons Act (CRIPA), a federal court could postpone action on an inmate civil rights case until the inmate exhausted his or her remedies under a grievance system if the system met certain standards and was approved by either the U.S. Department of Justice or the federal court. Relatively few jurisdictions took advantage of this law, probably because of objections to the content of the standards which a grievance system had to meet to be certified.

The PLRA expands the exhaustion requirement. Now, an inmate must exhaust any available grievance or appeal mechanism, not just one which meets federal standards. This means that if an inmate does not file a grievance about a matter, he or she probably will not be able to file a later civil rights case about the same matter.

Torts

A *tort* is defined as a civil (as opposed to criminal) wrong and arises when there is a violation of some duty that the defendant owes the plaintiff. A classic type of tort case is the suit that arises from the negligent operation of an automobile, in which the negligence of the defendant (the failure to use reasonable care) injures the plaintiff. The "duty" of the operator of the car is to show reasonable care in operating the automobile, so as not to endanger another person.

What amounts to "reasonable care" in a given situation sometimes is defined by state statute, but more often is defined by the courts through what is known as the common law. *The common law* is the law

31

that comes from the courts as they define and apply principles of custom and historic usage (as opposed to principles from laws passed by legislative bodies). The common law traces back to the fundamental principles and rules of action defined by the courts in England.

Tort actions common in corrections include such issues as the negligent loss of property, failure to protect the inmate from harm, medical malpractice, or breaches of other duties of reasonable care that correctional staff may owe inmates or others. Improper training, supervision, or assignment of staff also can be the basis of a negligence claim against a supervisor. In some states, victims of crimes committed by persons under some form of supervision (probation, parole, and so forth) are able to sue supervising officials and agencies under theories of negligent release or supervision.

A tort suit seeks only damages. It typically is filed in state court.

Often, a lawsuit about a particular subject, such as medical care, may be brought as either a tort or a civil rights claim. The legal burden the plaintiff may have to meet to win is often different between a tort and a civil rights claim, even when the operative facts in the case are exactly the same. For example, if an inmate feels he or she has received inadequate medical care, the claim in a tort suit would be one of negligence. But if a civil rights claim were brought, the claim would have to be "deliberate indifference to serious medical needs," a more difficult burden than showing simple negligence.

Inmates often prefer to file civil rights suits, even when the burden in those cases may be greater than in tort suits. There are several reasons for this.

1. Historically, federal courts (where civil rights cases are usually brought) are seen as more sympathetic to inmate claims than are state courts, the site of a tort suit.
2. The scope of possible relief in a civil rights case may be broader than in a tort. No injunctive relief is available in a tort. State law sometimes limits the amount of damages that can be awarded against government officials or may immunize those officials from damages altogether. Some states do not allow punitive damages. These limitations do not apply in civil rights cases.
3. Attorneys' fee awards, available in civil rights cases, are not available in tort suits.

Habeas Corpus

In a habeas corpus action, the petitioner claims that he or she is being held in custody illegally in violation of some constitutional right. A habeas corpus petition typically will not relate to anything a correctional employee did or did not do. Instead, it will attack an action of the court or agency responsible for the individual being in custody. Habeas corpus petitions name the custodian of the person as the respondent (defendant); therefore, the name of the warden of a prison frequently will appear on the pleadings.

Sometimes an inmate will challenge the results of a disciplinary hearing in a habeas corpus proceeding, in which case an individual employee could be involved directly with the case. Most states allow inmates to file some form of habeas corpus petition in state court. When an inmate can show he or she has "exhausted state remedies," a habeas corpus petition can be filed in federal court. While habeas corpus petitions become a form of appeal beyond normal appeal proceedings, they are limited to constitutional issues.

It is through habeas corpus petitions that persons under sentence of death repeatedly may challenge their death sentence. The only relief obtainable in a habeas corpus proceeding is release from custody.

State inmates filed nearly 19,000 habeas corpus petitions in federal court in 1998.[9] This is a sharp increase from a few years previous. The total number of habeas type proceedings filed in state courts is undoubtedly much higher.

Other Types of Lawsuits

These are not the only types of suits a correctional officer may see. An officer may be involved directly in personnel actions that can end up in court. Officers themselves may bring claims relating to discrimination on the basis of race, sex, disability, or other reason. Passage of the Americans with Disabilities Act (ADA) has resulted in many more claims brought by both officers and inmates concerning treatment of disabilities.

Conclusion

While perhaps 98 of every 100 civil rights actions filed by or on behalf of inmates against correctional personnel result in a judgment in favor of the defendant, civil rights actions and federal habeas corpus petitions have had a tremendous effect on the administration of corrections in America since the late 1960s. Entire correctional systems have been reformed pursuant to civil rights actions. Institution disciplinary processes take the form they do because of civil rights suits. Due process in parole and probation revocation proceedings is required because of the courts interpreting and applying constitutional principles. Other examples could be given at length to support the theory that civil rights actions probably have been the single greatest agent for change in corrections in this century.

The expansion of inmate rights has slowed—some would say it has even reversed itself to some degree—in recent years. The biggest factor in this change has been the increasingly conservative Supreme Court, which in decision after decision has chipped away at inmate rights. Passage of the Prison Litigation Reform Act, while not changing any substantive rights of inmates, should discourage inmates from filing as many lawsuits as they have been filing. As the federal courts become less receptive to inmate complaints, there may be a shift of inmate litigation from the federal courts to the state courts in which the inmate seeks relief under various provisions of state constitutions.

Review Questions

1. List three types of lawsuits most commonly filed by inmates.

2. True or false: A state cannot be sued directly in a civil rights action.

3. Give one example of when a supervisor could be held liable in a civil rights action, even if the supervisor did not take part directly in the actions that led to the suit.

Notes

1. *Monell v. Department of Social Services,* 98 S.Ct. 2018 (1978).
2. *West v. Atkins,* 487 U.S. 42 (1988).
3. *City of Canton v. Harris,* 109 S.Ct. 1197 (1989).
4. 18 USC § 3626(a).
5. Id.
6. *Lewis v. Casey,* 518 U.S. 343 (1996).

7. *Richardson v. McKnight*, 521 U.S. 399 (1997).

8. *Cleavinger v. Saxner*, 106 S.Ct. 496 (1986).

9. *Sourcebook of Criminal Justice Statistics*, 1999, p. 442. Department of Justice, Bureau of Justice Statistics.

IV.

Access to the Courts

The idea of anyone—inmate or free person—having rights of any kind becomes meaningless if there is no way the person can have the rights enforced. In any society, rules (which often translate into "rights") must govern the conduct and relations between people and organizations (including government). Conflicts will develop over whether these rules have been followed in a given situation. These disputes might range from an argument between two neighbors as to where the boundary line between their property lies, to arguments between a state and the federal government over whether a federal law unconstitutionally infringes on the state's sovereignty in some way. These disputes include questions of the relationship between inmates and the government agencies and employees that keep them in custody.

Some process is necessary to resolve these disputes, to decide if someone's rights have been violated by someone else, and if so, to then decide what should be done to remedy the situation. In America, our local, state, and federal court systems exist for this purpose. Without the courts or some similar dispute-resolving body with the power to enforce its decisions, rights would belong only to the strongest, and any freedoms "guaranteed" by laws or the Constitution would become hollow and often only illusory.

The courts are the branch of government whose primary function is determining if someone's rights (constitutional rights, statutory rights, and so forth) have been violated and, if so, what sort of remedy to allow. Because these duties may require judging the actions of government agencies and interpreting and evaluating laws, the courts exist as a separate branch of government, independent of the legislative and executive branches.

But having a court system to protect rights and resolve disputes will mean nothing if a person cannot get a dispute into court. So, while the

Constitution nowhere contains the phrase "access to the courts," the Supreme Court has long held that the right of access to the courts is inherently part of the concept of due process, if not other parts of the Constitution, as well.

Not only is there a constitutionally protected right of access to the courts, but that right is very important and fundamental, since all other rights may depend on a person being able to get to court. For persons not in custody, the right of access to the courts is seldom an issue. If individuals feel their rights have been violated, they can hire a lawyer and file a suit. Or, if they cannot afford a lawyer, they can research the law, prepare the suit themselves, and file it with the appropriate court.

Inmates' Access to the Courts

For persons in custody, the right of access to the courts is much more of an issue, since the institution literally can be a physical barrier between the inmate and lawyers, legal research materials, and the courts. The Supreme Court first began to recognize a right of access to the courts for inmates in 1941 in the *Hull* case: ". . . the state and its officers may not abridge or impair [an inmate's] right to apply to a federal court for a writ of habeas corpus."[1] This case arose because the State of Michigan had a policy that required any suit that an inmate wanted to file had to be approved by the lawyer for the state parole board, to be sure the suit was "in proper form." The Court said it was unconstitutional for the state to set up this sort of barrier between the inmate and the court.

A number of years later, a Tennessee policy prohibiting one inmate from helping another with a suit was challenged. The Supreme Court held in *Johnson v. Avery* that the prison may impose certain reasonable *limitations* and regulations on one inmate assisting another, but cannot prohibit such activity, at least until the prison provides reasonable alternative forms of assistance to the inmates.[2] "Writ-writers" or "jailhouse lawyers," inmates who help other inmates with suits, remain a fixture in correctional institutions.

The next time the Supreme Court looked at an access to the courts question was in 1974, in a case more famous for its holdings about inmate disciplinary hearings, *Wolff v. McDonnell*.[3] Buried in the last pages of the opinion, though, is discussion of the question of whether inmates' right of access to the courts pertained only to filing habeas corpus petitions (both the *Hull* and *Avery* cases involved just habeas corpus petitions) or whether the right included civil rights cases brought under 42 USC 1983. The court held the right included civil rights cases.

The fourth and by far the most important Supreme Court access to the courts case came in 1977 with *Bounds v. Smith*, when the Court went beyond saying the state could not impose barriers between inmates and the courts and instead said the state had an affirmative duty to assist inmates:

> . . . the fundamental constitutional right of access to the courts requires prison authorities to assist inmates in the preparation and filing of meaningful legal papers by providing prisoners with adequate law libraries or adequate assistance from persons trained in the law [emphasis added].[5]

The *Bounds* case involved a challenge to the resources the North Carolina Department of Corrections provided its inmates, who were scattered throughout the state in more than seventy different institutions, many of which were quite small.

By the time the case reached the Supreme Court, North Carolina had agreed to provide major libraries in several central locations and to move inmates to those libraries on request. The Supreme Court approved this plan and the contents of the libraries that North Carolina proposed.

The duty to provide "meaningful assistance" extends to jails, not just prisons, although what is required in jails may be slightly different in light of the relatively short time most inmates spend in jail. But for inmates in jail for periods of several months or more, the right probably is virtually identical.

In 1996, the Supreme Court revisited the area of access to the courts for the first time since its 1977 decision in *Bounds* in a case called *Lewis v. Casey*.[6] In this case, which involved the access to the courts system in the Arizona Department of Corrections, the Court generally reaffirmed the principle in *Bounds* that institutions have the affirmative duty to provide inmates with assistance in the form of law libraries or persons trained in the law. However, the Court also made it somewhat more difficult for inmates to sue successfully about denial of

39

their right of access to the courts by saying that to win such a claim, the inmate must prove he or she actually has been harmed ("prejudiced") in some way as a result of inadequate legal resources. An example of such harm would be if the inmate had a suit actually dismissed because of the inadequate resources available.

Case Study: Bounds Now Means Lawyers for North Carolina

The 1977 Supreme Court decision did not end the *Bounds* litigation. Almost a decade later, the parties again were back in court, with the issue then being whether North Carolina had complied with the plan approved by the Supreme Court in 1977. The District Court found North Carolina had not complied with the plan and ordered North Carolina to begin providing lawyers to assist inmates. The Court of Appeals affirmed this order, and the Supreme Court refused to hear the case again.[4] So, North Carolina, where a combination of libraries and an inmate transfer system were originally approved, now must provide lawyers, unlike virtually any other jurisdiction in the country because the state was not able to convince the lower courts that it had complied with its original commitments. This ruling has more to do with a court's power to issue orders to remedy a correctional problem than with the basic institutional duty to provide resources for inmates.

Typical of many inmate access to the courts cases after *Lewis* is the case of *Tourscher v. McCullough*.[7] The inmate complained that Pennsylvania prison officials violated his right of access to the courts by making him work in the prison cafeteria while his conviction was on appeal. Both the district court and court of appeals dismissed this argument. The court of appeals noted that Mr. Tourscher had failed to make any sort of a showing that his cafeteria work interfered with his ability to prosecute his appeal in state court. Absent a showing of this sort of injury, his case failed to state a claim.

Law Libraries and *Lewis v. Casey*—A Right Redefined

Under *Bounds*, and before *Lewis*, a very common access to the courts claim related to the adequacy of prison law libraries. Remember, *Bounds* had said one way prison officials could comply with their duty to provide some level of assistance to inmates was through law libraries. Most prisons and jails chose to try to meet their *Bounds* obligations through providing law libraries in some form, instead of providing "assistance from persons trained in the law," another alternative mentioned in *Bounds*.

Courts commonly required agencies to buy very substantial law libraries, costing tens of thousands of dollars to purchase and thousands every year to maintain. Along with lawsuits about what should be in the library were claims about such things as how much access time had to be provided, the adequacy of the space where the books were kept, and how access could be provided to inmates in segregated units, who could not physically come to the library. A number of cases held that book paging and delivery systems for segregated units were not acceptable.[8]

Law libraries considered adequate under standards courts used before *Lewis* might be available in major prisons or large jails, but typically were not available in smaller facilities.

As institutions increased their reliance on books, questions began to arise around how the most complete law library could provide adequate access to the courts for the inmate who could not read. Since many prison inmates are illiterate, or have very limited reading skills, this became a serious question. The author of this book served as an expert witness in one case in which the prison system was investing substantial amounts of time and effort in trying to provide trained inmate law clerks who, it was felt, could provide assistance to the illiterate inmate.

The affirmative duties for correctional administrators that began in *Bounds* seemed to just keep growing. This growth perhaps reached its zenith in *Lewis*, and in doing so, proved to be the straw that may have broken the camel's back. The district court in *Lewis* found that the access to the courts system that the Arizona Department of Corrections provided its inmates was not sufficient. Inadequacies related to such things as the training of library staff, updating legal materials, and photocopying. Specially affected by the inadequacies were inmates segregated from the main prison population, and illiterate or non-English speaking inmates. Most of the court's negative conclusions where not based on evidence that inmates had been harmed, but rather on the idea that inmates might at some point be harmed in pursuing a legal claim.

Although the trial only showed two inmates who had been actually injured by inadequacies in the Arizona system, the court ordered systemwide relief. The court appointed a special master to assist the court in formulating a plan for relief. After eight months, he produced what became, with minor changes, a court-ordered blueprint for the operation of the access to the courts system. The plan went into minute detail, including the number of hours law libraries were to be kept open, the content of a video course for training inmate law clerks, and the educational requirements for prison librarians.

When *Lewis* reached the Supreme Court, a majority of the Court did not welcome the result with open arms. The Court reversed the lower court decision. In doing so, the Court changed the way courts must analyze access to the courts claims, encouraged innovations other than the traditional law library, and was extremely critical of the lower court's detailed order. At one point, the opinion notes ". . . the injunction imposed by the District Court was inordinately— indeed wildly— intrusive."[9] *Lewis* then becomes an important case both for access to the courts issues and for questions regarding court injunctive orders in reform cases.

The "actual injury" requirement from *Lewis* makes it harder for inmates to win access to the courts claims. It is now common to see access to the courts cases dismissed because the inmate failed to show he suffered harm or prejudice caused by the institution's law library or other access to the courts program.

Lewis also puts other limits on the right of access to the courts. The case makes it clear that the right of access to the courts protects the inmate's ability to challenge his criminal conviction or prison conditions and practices. It does not protect the inmate's ability to seek judicial relief for other matters, such as pursuing parenting or child custody claims, which may be important to some inmates. "In other words, [the right of access to the courts] does not guarantee inmates the wherewithal to transform themselves into litigating engines capable of filing everything from shareholder derivative actions to skip-and-fall claims."[10] In saying this, the Supreme Court did not mean that inmates are barred from filing such claims, only that the prison has no constitutional duty to help them do so.

Case Study: Inmates Can Wear Out Welcome to the Courts

Inmate Debro Siddig Abdul-Akbar filed suit complaining about various alleged problems of obtaining access to the courts. But rather than having the court smooth out these problems for the inmate, he found the court actually putting up barriers to his filing more lawsuits.

The inmate had filed more than forty civil suits in a seven-year period. In response to the latest one, the district court dismissed the case as frivolous and ordered the court clerk to refuse to file any more cases for Abdul-Akbar unless he met certain extraordinary requirements. The court of appeals agreed such restrictions were appropriate in cases where there was a history of an inmate abusing the privilege of bringing a lawsuit in forma pauperis.[13]

But having said that Abdul-Akbar's history of abusing the in forma pauperis privilege justified such an injunction, the court reversed the lower court's dismissal of his latest lawsuit, saying the allegations in the complaint, if true, might state a claim for relief. *Abdul-Akbar v. Watson*, 901 F.2d 329 (3rd Cir., 1990).

Lewis adds another important limit on the duty of prisons and jails under *Bounds*. The affirmative duty to provide assistance in some form only extends to allow the inmate to bring a grievance to court, not necessarily to discover if he has a grievance nor to litigate effectively once a case gets to court.

The problem of dealing with the illiterate inmate remains after *Lewis*. The opinion notes the problem, but does not address it in any way. However, it remains obvious that any access to the courts system that relies on an inmate's ability to read, whether it be legal forms, or sophisticated legal treatises, cannot help the inmate who cannot read. Sooner or later, such an inmate will have a nonfrivolous legal claim of the sort protected by *Lewis* and will not be able to bring that claim if he or she cannot find some form of assistance. What form that assistance must take remains to be decided in future lawsuits.

Perhaps the most significant aspect of *Lewis* is one that is slow to develop. The opinion clearly states that *Bounds*, as interpreted by *Lewis*, does not create an inmate's right to a law library. The Court encourages agencies to experiment with other means of providing assistance, suggesting that a combination of minimal access to legal advice and to legal forms might be enough. At least some agencies have moved to replace their law libraries with this type of program, but there is not yet a body of lower court decisions that analyze this approach.

Questions about law libraries long have been the subject of extensive litigation. The meaning of the right of access to the courts seemed to be constantly expanding. *Lewis* puts the brakes on this expansion. The case allows agencies to reexamine how they provide inmates with legal assistance and forces courts to take a different, more conservative approach in defining the details of the right of access to the courts.

Dealing with the Litigious Inmate

Some inmates seem to make a career out of filing lawsuits. One Washington State inmate filed more than 200 lawsuits in a five-year period.[11] Every state has a similar example. Courts have concluded that at least some of these litigious inmates file suits primarily as a means of harassing and vexing both the court and the correctional employees named as defendants.[12]

Why can't something be done about this abuse of the legal process? Why don't the courts just dismiss cases without requiring the government to invest the time and money necessary to respond? Why can't institutions take action against inmates for filing suits that have no merit by disciplining them or denying them privileges?

Over the years, some courts have tried to impose some limitations on litigious inmates. These have included requiring inmates with some funds to pay at least part of the filing fees normally charged a person wishing to file a lawsuit in federal district court (the filing fee is now $120). In cases of extreme abuse, courts may try to limit the number of suits the inmate can file or set other extraordinary requirements for an inmate to proceed with a suit. However, these efforts have been sporadic and have had little or no impact on the steady increase of inmate suits (inmate civil rights filings generally have increased at about the same rate at which the total inmate population has increased over recent years).

The Prison Litigation Reform Act (PLRA) attacks the "frequent filer" problem in a couple of ways. The requirement that inmates pay filing fees on the time payment plan (as opposed to waiving fees altogether) should deter some inmates from being as quick to file a lawsuit as perhaps was the case in the past. Remember, the filing fee changes allow, indeed require, institution officials to withdraw funds from the inmate's account and send them to the court to pay a filing fee debt. The system does not depend on the inmate choosing to send money.

The three strikes provision of the PLRA hinders the frequent filer even more directly by barring inmates from filing future cases after three cases have been dismissed as frivolous, malicious, or failing to state a claim. Many inmate cases are dismissed on the latter ground, so the inmates who file one case after another are likely to work themselves quickly into a three strikes status. The exception to the three strikes rule, where there is a showing the inmate is in "imminent danger of serious physical injury" should not prove to be a major loophole in the three strikes law.

When an inmate files a lawsuit that names a staff member as a defendant in a lawsuit, which seeks millions of dollars in damages, especially when the staff member may realize the suit has little or no merit, there is a natural tendency to want to "get back" at the inmate in some way. But regardless of the merits (or lack thereof) of the original suit, retaliation against an inmate for filing a lawsuit violates the inmate's right of access to the courts. Doing so would punish individuals for exercising their constitutional rights. Just as the institution may not set up barriers between inmates and the courts before lawsuits are filed, the institution may not penalize the inmate for filing a lawsuit.

Attorney Visits

Courts unanimously have recognized the right of a lawyer to visit a client in prison. This also includes the right of persons working for a lawyer, such as investigators or law clerks, to visit inmate clients of the lawyer.

While the institution can impose reasonable regulations on when lawyers may visit, the key word is "reasonable." Any such limitations should be flexible and recognize the legitimate need for access outside normal working hours (when the lawyer may be in trial). Communication between lawyer and client is privileged, and institution staff may not eavesdrop on such conversations.

Indigence

Where an inmate is indigent, the institution must provide reasonable amounts of postage and supplies (paper, pens, and so forth) for the inmate wishing to exercise the right of access to the courts.[14] A problem may arise in defining indigence for purposes of deciding when an inmate is entitled to stamps. Again, rules in this area need to be flexible. Most courts have said inmates do not have a right of access to copy machines.[15]

Appointed Counsel

There are a variety of issues that arise from time to time under the general duty of providing inmates with "meaningful" access to the courts. What about appointed counsel? Many jail inmates are represented by lawyers in their pending criminal cases. Do these lawyers, often paid for by the state, provide adequate access to the courts? Probably not.

The fact that a jail inmate has a lawyer appointed in his or her criminal case will not assure the inmate is being provided "meaningful access to the courts" under *Bounds*, because often the appointed counsel will not be able to provide the inmate with any advice or assistance outside the criminal case. Even where appointed counsel arguably do provide meaningful access to the courts for their clients, this still leaves the jail with the need to provide resources for the sentenced inmates housed in the jail, who no longer are represented by counsel.

Conclusion

The right of access to the courts has proven controversial in practice. In theory, it is hard to argue against the concept that someone should be able to file a lawsuit which claims their rights under the Constitution have been violated. While some very important decisions in corrections began with one inmate filing a lawsuit by himself or herself, the tens of thousands of inmate claims dismissed by federal courts every year without even a trial, perhaps without even a response from defendants, shows how little merit most inmate suits have. Courts have been very reluctant to take steps that might check the flow of inmate lawsuits. Congress, in passing the Prison Litigation Reform Act, has stepped in where courts have not in an attempt to cut down on the number of inmate civil rights claims. As the twenty-first century begins, the total number of inmate civil rights claims filed in federal court has decreased sharply.

Review Questions

1. Why is the right of access to the courts an important part of America's legal system?

2. If an inmate is represented by appointed counsel in a criminal case, why is this not necessarily sufficient access to the courts?

3. What is the major vulnerability of an access to the courts system which is built around books and other written materials?

Notes

1. *Ex Parte Hull*, 312 U.S. 546 (1941).
2. *Johnson v. Avery*, 393 U.S. 483 (1969).
3. 418 U.S. 539 (1974), *see* Chapter 6.
4. *Smith v. Bounds*, 813 F.2d 1299 (1979).
5. *Bounds v. Smith*, 430 U.S. 817 (1977).
6. *Lewis v. Casey*, 116 S. Ct. 2174 (1996).
7. 184 F.3d 236 (3rd Cir., 1999).
8. *Touissaint v. McCarthy*, 597 F.Supp. 1388 (C.D. Cal., 1985).
9. 116 S.Ct. at 2185.
10. 116 S.Ct. at 2182.
11. *Demos v. Kincheloe*, E.D. Wash., #C-80-152, 1984 (unpublished).
12. *Doe v. State*, E.D. Wash., #C-83-409-JLQ, 1984 (unpublished).
13. Literally, "in the form or manner of a pauper." When any plaintiff (inmate or not) can establish he or she is indigent and (at least in federal court) the suit does not appear to be

frivolous or malicious, the normal filing fees are waived. Most inmates are granted *in forma pauperis* status.

14. PLRA Section 805, 28 USC Section 1915 A.
15. *Gittens v. Sullivan*, 848 F.2d 389 (2d Cir., 1988).

V.
Inmate Rights Versus Institutional Interests: The Balancing Test

Many legal battles between inmates and jails or prisons center on a conflict between the right the inmate is claiming and a competing interest of the institution.

1. An inmate wants to be able to wear a special religious medallion that, outside the institutional setting, would be of no concern to anyone. But prison officials are concerned that the medallion could be used as a weapon.
2. Another inmate wants to receive a publication on martial arts techniques. Outside the facility, the publication might sell on a street corner newsstand. But prison officials are concerned about inmates teaching themselves martial arts and using what they learn either against each other or against officers.
3. An inmate whose religious and personal beliefs require a great deal of modesty wants to avoid being seen in the nude by strangers, including staff. He is particularly offended at the thought of being seen by women while using the toilet. But the institution requires inmates to be strip searched in certain circumstances and is using an increasing number of female officers as part of an equal opportunity program.

All of these conflicts—and many others—may wind up in court. And the court will be asked to decide whether the inmates' constitutionally protected interests in exercising their freedom of religion, freedom of the press, the right to be free from unreasonable searches (or right to privacy) are outweighed by the concerns expressed by the institution.

Despite the absolute language of much of the Bill of Rights (such as part of the First Amendment: "Congress shall make no law respecting the establishment of religion, or prohibiting the free exercise thereof . . ."), it is clear that constitutional rights are not absolute. The government can limit the exercise of rights in certain situations. The dimensions of a particular right (such as the protection from unreasonable searches) varies from one situation to another. But because "constitutional rights—fundamental rights of all persons in this country—are being restricted, the government must show a strong need to impose restrictions.

The challenge for the courts is to resolve disputes between persons desiring to exercise their rights in some way and the government's occasional desire to restrict that exercise. The court resolving such conflicts must balance the competing interests—the right versus the government's justification for its restriction—and decide which is the stronger. When is the government's concern strong enough to justify restricting someone from exercising a right guaranteed by the Constitution?

This sort of balancing approach has been a part of prisoners' rights litigation from its beginnings in the late 1960s. But surprisingly, the Supreme Court had hardly ever addressed how inmate rights should be weighed against institutional interests until the late 1980s. Then, in a series of cases decided between 1987 and early 1990, the Court addressed the question and developed a fundamental approach for analyzing the inmate right versus institutional interest conflicts. This test applies to all such questions, regardless of what particular constitutional right is involved.

Prior to this series of cases, lower courts were busy developing their own balancing tests. Unfortunately, different courts developed different tests, some of which strongly favored the constitutional right and required a very strong, clear showing of need by the institution to justify any restriction of the right. Other courts went in the opposite direction, adopting tests that favored the institutional interests.

The result of this lower court activity was confusion and uncertainty. Depending on what legal test was applied to a given set of facts (such as a rule requiring short hair and no beards), one court might approve the rule while another would find it an unconstitutional infringement on the inmate's religious rights guaranteed by the First Amendment.

The uncertainty began to be clarified in 1987 with two decisions by the Supreme Court.[1] The facts of one clearly demonstrate the rule the Court adopted and how that rule is to be applied.

50

O'Lone v. Estate of Shabazz

In *O'Lone v. Estate of Shabazz*, a number of Muslim inmates at a medium-security prison in New Jersey challenged a rule that prohibited them from attending Juum'ah, the basic congregational service in their faith. The inmates were in a custody status called "gang minimum," which required them to leave the walled portion of the prison every day to work in gangs outside the institution. Each group of eight to fifteen workers was supervised by one officer.

Under religious law, Juum'ah services only could be held at a specific time, when the gang minimum inmates were outside the facility. A Juum'ah service was held in the prison, but the inmates could not get to it unless excused from their work details and escorted back to the prison.

After problems arose with inmates coming off the work crews and back to the institution at odd times during the day, the institution adopted a rule that said inmates in gang minimum work would spend all day outside the institution, absent an emergency. Thus, the conflict was created: the inmates wanted to exercise their First Amendment religious beliefs by attending an important religious service. But the institution did not allow this to happen, citing various reasons, most of which related to security.

The history of *Shabazz* shows why a Supreme Court ruling in this area was needed. The trial court ruled in favor of the institution, relying on a legal test defined earlier by the Third Circuit Court of Appeals. The case then was appealed to the Third Circuit, which decided its earlier case set too easy a standard. The Third Circuit reset its scales, balanced the inmates' rights and institutional interests, and reversed the trial court decision. To justify the restrictions, the institution would have to show not only that the restriction furthered its security interests, but also that no reasonable method existed under which the inmates' religious freedoms could be accommodated.

The Supreme Court disagreed with the approach the court of appeals had taken, and particularly with the "no reasonable method of accommodation" requirement. The Court said: "When a prison regulation impinges on inmates' constitutional rights, the regulation is valid if it is reasonably related to legitimate penological interests." Earlier, and in other decisions, the Court identified legitimate penological interests as including deterrence of crime, rehabilitation of offenders, and institutional security.

The phrase "reasonably related to legitimate penological interests" is vague and subjective. Standing alone, it provides little guidance to persons running correctional facilities. Fortunately, the Court did not stop with this phrase, but went on to spell out a four-step process for applying the test. This process is relatively clear and does provide a blueprint for administrators to use in decisions that may involve the restriction of inmates' constitutional rights.

1. Is there a valid, rational connection (a reasonable or logical connection) between the restriction (in this case, the rule prohibiting some inmates from attending Juum'ah) and legitimate interests of the institution? In *Shabazz*, the Court found such connections do exist, both in regard to security and rehabilitative interests.

2. Are there other ways the inmate has of exercising the right in question? In other words, given that the inmates could not attend the religious service, could they exercise their religious beliefs in other ways? Noting the inmates could attend other Muslim services, had access to an Imam (a Muslim religious leader), and were able to have special religious-sensitive diets, the Court found there were alternatives.

3. If the right is accommodated, what impact will that have on staff, other inmates, and on institution resources? Will there be a "ripple effect" on others? The Court found various potentially negative impacts on resources, institution safety, and security. In this area, the Court said that particular deference should be given by lower courts to the judgments and concerns of prison administrators.

4. Finally, the reasonableness of a restriction tends to be shown if there are no ready (obvious, easy) alternatives that would accommodate the inmates' interest at a minimal cost to the institution. Here the Court could see no such alternatives.

After applying each of the four steps to the facts of the *Shabazz* case, the Court upheld the restrictions.

Shabazz actually was the second of two 1987 cases in which the Court announced and applied this test. In the other case, *Turner v. Safley*, regulations prohibiting inmate-to-inmate mail and virtually prohibiting inmate marriages were challenged. Using the same four-step approach, the Court upheld the mail restrictions but overturned the marriage rule. The Court suggested that a more narrowly drawn rule regulating inmate marriages might be satisfactory.

Case Study: Apply Restrictions Equally, Be Sure of Reasons for Restrictions

Successfully defending a restriction of an inmate's ability to practice his or her religion may depend on whether the policy is enforced consistently. For instance, requiring a Rastafarian to cut his long hair (his "dreadlocks") while allowing Native Americans to wear their hair long was of concern to one court.[2] Another court expressed similar concerns in a case where the inmate who asserted a religious belief in long hair argued that other religious groups in the institution, including Sikhs and Native Americans, were not required to cut their hair. The court in that case also was concerned that there was no evidence produced by the defendants to show that the interests they asserted to justify their short hair policy were, in fact, the reasons that the policy was adopted.[3]

The following are two points about these decisions to keep in mind:

1. The Court clearly rejected any notion that the institution must prove that no reasonable alternative exists that would accommodate an inmate's constitutional interest. The test the Court adopted is a comparatively easy one for the institution to meet.
2. In evaluating an institution's reasons for imposing a restriction, a reviewing court is to give considerable deference to the judgment of correctional officials. It should not second-guess the concerns of officials.

Turner and *Shabazz* Extended

At first, there was some question as to how broadly the *"Turner* test" (as the rule has come to be known) would be applied. An answer to this question came in 1989, when the Court again applied the *Turner* test, this time in a case involving the censorship or rejection of publications sent to an institution.[4]

Under attack were rules of the Federal Bureau of Prisons, which spelled out the circumstances under which an institution could refuse to admit a publication. Typical of these rules was one that prohibited material that "depicts, encourages, or describes methods of escape from correctional facilities . . . ." The court of appeals had thrown out two-thirds of this rule (the "depicts" and "describes" portions) since that court felt publications to be rejected actually must encourage or advocate security breaches, or at least be likely to create such a breach.

The Supreme Court reversed the lower court and held that it had applied too stringent a standard in judging the rules. In reaching this conclusion, the Court overruled a portion of one of its first prison cases, which also dealt with mail rules and which many people felt set the ground rules for any mail restrictions.[5]

The Court limited its earlier decision to dealing with outgoing mail and said the *Turner* test applied to all incoming correspondence, including both publications and letters (except legal mail; *see* Chapter 7). Under the *Turner* test, the rules were valid.

In early 1990, the Court made it absolutely clear that the Turner test should be followed in every case that involves trying to balance an inmate's constitutional rights against legitimate penological interests (which will be security, in the great majority of instances).[6]

In the case in question, called *Washington v. Harper*,[7] the issues dealt with involuntarily medicating mentally ill inmates and arose under the Due Process Clause of the Fourteenth Amendment. The Court applied the *Turner* test in ruling in favor of the state and said *Turner* applied, no matter what Amendment the inmate was suing under, and even if not every part of the four-step approach could be applied.

Therefore, *Turner* now governs not only First Amendment issues (such as religious practice questions or publication rejection issues), but also issues arising under the Fourth Amendment (searches), Eighth Amendment (cruel and unusual punishment), and the Fourteenth

Amendment (due process), if the right the inmate is claiming is seen as running counter to some conflicting interest of the institution (security, safety, rehabilitation). In some of these areas, the application of the *Turner* rule may result in changes of old legal precedents, which were decided under different legal tests.

The following are some examples of cases decided since *Turner* in which institutional restrictions were approved:

1. Two inmates were transferred from a lower to a high security prison based on association with violent extremist groups, where the association had occurred ten years before the transfer. The inmates had done nothing recently to raise concerns about their security. The district court decided officials had exaggerated their response to security concerns, but the court of appeals reversed, approving the transfer.[8]
2. A Jewish inmate attacked a rule limiting beards to no more than one inch. He won the case at the district court before *Turner*. The district court reconsidered the case after *Turner* and again threw out the rule. On appeal, the court of appeals reversed the lower court and upheld the rule.[9]

In another case very similar to the *Shabazz* case, a handful of Jewish inmates were not allowed to move between institutions in a prison complex to attend religious services, even though such movement had been allowed in the past without problem. In this case, the court felt there were easy alternatives to what amounted to a total ban on the inmates being able to attend important services and therefore required the institution to move the inmates for the services.[10]

Conclusion

The *Turner* version balancing test has the effect of presetting the scale a court will use to weigh competing constitutional and institutional interests and to preset that scale somewhat in favor of the institution. In other words, while the institution will still have to convince a reviewing court that a restriction it is imposing furthers a legitimate penological interest, that burden will not be that difficult to meet. More and more courts will approve such restrictions, giving increasing deference to the judgment and concerns of prison officials.

Review Questions

1. What is the most common institutional concern that may justify restriction of an inmate's constitutional rights?

2. True or false: The *Turner* test has made it harder for an institution to justify restricting constitutional rights of inmates.

3. The institution imposes a restriction on an inmate practicing his religion. The inmate sues, claiming his First Amendment rights have been violated. The institution responds by saying, "The restriction was imposed because of security needs." Based on this response, will the institution win the lawsuit? Why or why not?

Notes

1. *Turner v. Safley*, 107 S.Ct. 2254 (1987). *O'Lone v. Estate of Shabazz*, 107 S.Ct. 2400 (1987).
2. *Reed v. Faulkner*, 842 F.2d 906 (2d Cir., 1988).
3. *Swift v. Lewis*, 901 F.2d 730 (9th Cir., 1990).
4. *Thornburgh v. Abbott*, 109 S.Ct. 1874 (1989).
5. *Procunier v. Martinez*, 94 S.Ct. 1800 (1974).
6. *Washington v. Harper*, 449 U.S. 210 (1990);110 S.Ct. 1028 (1990).
7. Id. 449 U.S. 210 (1990).
8. *Baraldini v. Thornburgh*, 884 F.2d 615 (D.C. Cir., 1989).
9. *Fromer v. Scully*, 874 F.2d 69 (2d Cir., 1989).
10. *Whitney v. Brown*, 882 F.2d 1068 (6th Cir., 1989).

VI.

The First Amendment: Religion, Mail, Publications, Visiting, and Expression

The First Amendment to the U.S. Constitution provides freedom of religion, of speech, and of the press.

> Congress shall make no law respecting an establishment of religion, or prohibiting the free exercise thereof, or abridging the freedom of speech, or of the press; or the right of the people peaceably to assemble, and to petition the government for a redress of grievances.

The First Amendment is perhaps the most cherished and fundamental freedom in the Bill of Rights. Freedom of religion, speech, and of the press are recognized as absolutely basic parts of the structure of American society.

But even though the First Amendment says no law may be made restricting or abridging the rights guaranteed by the Amendment, over the years, courts have recognized that in certain situations, the government legitimately may restrict rights protected by the First Amendment. In general, such restrictions are very difficult for the government to justify: a "clear and present danger" may have to be shown before the government can prevent someone in the general public from exercising his or her First Amendment rights.

Prior restraint—preventing someone from exercising a right as opposed to responding to the way the right was exercised—is not favored. The purposes of the First Amendment are better served by letting someone make the speech or hold the demonstration and then responding to problems created by those acts than forbidding the acts altogether based on a concern that they might cause problems.

But the burden to restrict First Amendment rights inside a correctional institution is not this great because the government's legitimate need is to be able to run a safe, secure facility. Therefore, a person's First Amendment rights actually are reduced, sometimes very substantially, by the fact of being incarcerated.

First Amendment Rights in Prisons and Jails

First Amendment issues, particularly religious questions, were among the first and remain among the most common corrections issues that courts have dealt with over the years.

As with other constitutional rights, inmates are protected by the First Amendment while in custody, but the protections are considerably less than they would be on the streets. In other words, the institution still must justify a restriction on an inmate's First Amendment rights, but that justification is much easier to make than it would be outside the institution setting.

Most First Amendment issues arise because of the way in which the inmate wants to exercise a First Amendment right (such as receipt of a publication) conflicts with some interest of the institution. As such, they are resolved now through the balancing test, described in Chapter V. Under this approach, a court will approve the decision to restrict an inmate's exercise of a First Amendment right if the court finds the restriction is reasonably related to a "legitimate penological interest" of the institution.[1] The most common of such interests are security and safety, but rehabilitation and deterrence of crime also have been recognized as legitimate penological interests.

Interests that usually are not seen as being strong enough to justify restricting inmates' constitutional rights are ones relating to providing administrative convenience, saving money, and resulting in overall efficiency. But if these sorts of interests can be tied to interests of security, then they may be seen as legitimate.

Other Religious Issues

Some legal issues surrounding religion do not involve the balancing test because they do not directly involve a conflict between the inmate's religious practices and any interest of the institution.

What is a religion?

If something is a religion, then an inmate's attempts to practice the religion usually only can be restricted if the restriction can be justified under the *Turner* balancing test. On the other hand, if something is *not* a religion, then the institution usually will not legally have to justify restrictions, since the practice will not be seen as being protected by the First Amendment. So, sometimes it is in the interest of institution officials to try to decide if something is or is not a religion.

This decision is not an easy one. Courts use different tests for deciding if something is a religion and hence protected by the First Amendment. One court used a somewhat objective test:

> a religion addresses fundamental and ultimate questions having to do with deep and imponderable matters . . . a religion is comprehensive in nature, (consisting) of a belief system as opposed to an isolated teaching . . . religion can often be recognized by the presence of certain formal and external signs.[2]

Another court defined religion as follows:

> . . . the feelings, acts, and experiences of individual men in their solitude, so far as they apprehend themselves to stand in relations to whatever they may consider the divine.[3]

The tests are difficult to understand, let alone apply in a particular situation. Yet, the test a court uses may dictate the result. For instance, the objective test from the *Africa* case was used in a criminal case in which the defendant claimed he was the Reverend of the Church of Marijuana. He said he sincerely believed that his religion commanded him to use, possess, and distribute marijuana for the benefit of mankind and the planet earth and that to prosecute him criminally would violate his First Amendment rights. The court said that while he may be sincere in his beliefs, they did not amount to a religion.[4] But how would this case have been decided if the court had used the more subjective test, where the inquiry is "whether the beliefs professed by a [claimant] are sincerely held and whether they are, in his own scheme of things, religious."?[5]

Another court, applying an objective test which in essence asked "does it look like a religion?" found that witchcraft, as practiced by the Church of Wicca, was a religion and that prison officials would have to justify any restrictions on its practice. The court found various restrictions imposed were justified.[6]

59

Sometimes the "what is a religion?" question arises in rather contrived situations, such as the inmate who formed the "Church of the New Song" (CONS). Among the early practices of this "religion" was a sacrament requiring the inmate to be served steak and wine from time to time. CONS was the subject of a great deal of litigation through the 1970s, with the courts eventually refusing to grant First Amendment protections to the Church of the New Song. More recently, this inmate was still litigating about something called the Holy Mizanic faith.[7]

Another court ruled that the Universal Life Church, which bestows religious titles ("Doctor of Divinity," and so forth) for a fee by mail, is not a religion.[8] Given the complexity of deciding whether something is or is not a religion and the lawsuits that may come from deciding something is not a religion, this decision is not one that line staff should make.

Just because an officer knows nothing about what an inmate offers as a religion, or the inmate's beliefs are very different from those held by the officer does not mean that what the inmate is trying to practice is not a religion. Regardless of what legal test courts use to decide if something is or is not a religion, they will not attempt to evaluate the merits of what is asserted to be a religion, or whether its beliefs are the "right" ones.

Sincerity of belief

If an inmate is not sincere in his or her religious beliefs, the institution is under no duty to accommodate the inmate's request to practice the religion. In one case, prison officials refused to allow an inmate a prayer rug until he asked for a pork-free diet. (The Muslim or Islamic faith believes its adherents should not eat or handle pork products.) In another case, failing to request religious services for twelve years, failing to submit information about the religion to the institution in response to a request, failing to file an administrative appeal about being denied religious services, and the generally ambiguous nature of the alleged religious beliefs all contributed to a finding of insincerity.[9]

One factor that courts generally have not accepted as indicating insincerity is the fact that the inmate's criminal actions are inconsistent with any sort of religious belief. The inmate's conduct while in prison will be a far more important determining factor about the inmate's sincerity (or lack of sincerity). Like the "what is a religion?" question, decisions that an inmate is not sincere and therefore may be denied permission to practice his or her religion in some way are not decisions that line staff should make. Sincerity of belief issues have not often been litigated.

State-paid chaplains

The First Amendment prohibits the state from "establishing" a religion. Taken literally, this bars the state from spending any taxpayer funds for religious activities. Yet, larger jails and prisons routinely hire chaplains. And courts have approved this practice, in part at least because where the state imposes burdens on someone freely practicing their religion (by incarcerating them or sending them around the world in the military), the state may compensate by spending money for religious purposes.[10] If state-paid chaplains actively proselytize inmates to join a particular faith, this could be seen as violating the prohibition against the state establishing a religion.

Allocation of resources

A large institution may have inmates belonging to a large number of different religious faiths. Must resources be allocated equally between these various groups, even though some groups may have a large number of adherents while others may have relatively few members? So long as the groups have a reasonable opportunity to practice their religions, courts have not held equality of treatment is required.[11]

Special diets

An area where some accommodation of religious practices is common is with special religious diets. Where there is a significant number of inmates with special religious dietary needs (such as not eating pork), courts favor accommodating the diet, at least through providing the inmates with enough variety of foods to allow the inmates to obtain a nutritionally adequate diet without violating their religious beliefs.

In 1998, a court went beyond requiring simply a pork-free diet for Jewish inmates in a state prison system, holding that the First Amendment required that prison officials provide Jewish inmates with a diet which not only was sufficient to sustain them in good health, but also did not violate kosher laws. The court approved a cold kosher diet, over the inmate's argument in favor of hot food.[12]

However, in extreme situations, where a very few inmates are demanding a particular diet and/or accommodating the diet would impose undue financial and administrative demands on the institution, courts have not required the dietary demands to be met. A concern that accommodating one special diet request would lead to a proliferation of similar claims justified denying the request.[13]

Case Study: Rastafarian Diet Too Complicated

A New York federal court refused to order the New York Department of Correctional Services to meet the dietary needs of Rastafarians. (Rastafarianism is a religion with roots in the culture of Jamaica.) The demands were quite complex and included things such as no meat, sometimes (depending on the sect) no canned foods or dairy products, no foods treated with nonorganic pesticides or fertilizers, and food only cooked in natural materials, such as clay pots.

It made no difference to the court that the prison system provided Orthodox Jewish inmates with Kosher or neutral diets and some special dietary accommodations for Muslims. The complexity of the Rastafarian's dietary requirements and the financial and administrative burdens that those requirements would create justified the differences (*Benjamin v. Coughlin*, 708 F.Supp. 570 (S.D.N.Y., 1989)).

Mail and Publications

Rejecting incoming mail

In 1989, the Supreme Court decided *Abbot v. Thornburgh*, a case dealing with another First Amendment issue: the censorship or rejection of incoming mail. Several lower courts had decided that to censor or reject publications, the institution had to show the material actually advocated some sort of security breach or was likely to cause a breach.

Thus, one court had thrown out rules of the Federal Bureau of Prisons, which allowed material to be rejected that "depicted or described" such things as methods of escape or activities that may lead to the use of physical violence or group disruption. The court did so by relying on a 1974 Supreme Court decision, which it felt controlled the issue.[14]

Again, the Supreme Court reversed the lower court and upheld the rule. The Court limited its 1974 case only to outgoing correspondence and said that for publications and other general (nonlegal) correspondence, the *Turner* test would apply. In other words, if censorship or rejection of a publication was "reasonably related to a legitimate penological objective," the restriction would be valid.

Now, incoming correspondence is judged by the same standard that applies to restrictions on such things as inmates' attempts to practice their religion, which in some way may conflict with legitimate institutional interests (security, in a very broad sense, and rehabilitation). Another important aspect of the Supreme Court's 1989 publication censorship case was the Court's holding that when any part of a publication was properly rejected, the entire issue of the publication could be rejected. Institution officials do not have to cut and paste magazines to review objectionable parts and deliver what is left. (The lower court had imposed a cut-and-paste requirement.)

The mail restriction rule applied

There have not been many publication rejection decisions since the Supreme Court's decision in the *Abbott* case. Racist literature, which could fan the flames of racial unrest in an institution, generally can be banned. At least some types of sexual publications also can be banned, but a ban on all sexually oriented publications may go too far.[15] There simply are too few court decisions regarding sexually oriented publications to be able to say with confidence where lines may be drawn regarding this type of publication.

A ban on pretrial detainees receiving any publications in the mail was upheld in one case, in part because of the relatively short time a detainee is likely to be in jail.[16]

For many years, there were very few court decisions dealing with the censorship of sexually oriented publications. While there were cases which approved of prison officials not allowing inmates to have extreme sorts of publications, such as publications which advocate sexual contact between men and boys,[17] there were not many cases dealing with more common types of publications such as *Playboy*. In the late 1990s, courts have addressed bans on this type of publication, and generally upheld the bans. For instance, a ban on publications showing frontal nudity was approved by the Ninth Circuit.[18] Another court approved a similar regulation, although it was more carefully drawn so as to limit its effect to publications which were sexual or erotic in nature, not something like *National Geographic*.[19]

Publication censorship decisions remain a very sensitive legal area. Agency rules and policies need to be drafted carefully, and the actual decision to reject a publication needs to be made by an official who understands the rules and their importance. The decision to reject a publication or a letter normally would not be made by line staff.

Due process and rejection

Rejection of publications or letters, either incoming or outgoing, also raises a due process issue. To help assure that rejection decisions are made fairly and according to proper standards, the Supreme Court requires the following when a publication or letter is rejected:

- The inmate must be given notice of the rejection (regardless of whether the inmate was the sender or the intended recipient of the letter).
- The author of the letter must be given an opportunity to protest the censorship decision to an official other than the person who made the original decision to reject the correspondence. This obviously requires that notice of the rejection also be given to the sender of the letter, if the sender is not an inmate.[20]

What if it is not a letter which is rejected, but a publication? Must a notice of rejection be sent to the publisher? In a case arising from the Virginia Department of Corrections, a district court said that notice to the inmate was enough. However, the court of appeals reversed, saying that since the inmate had never seen the publication which was rejected, he could hardly be in a position to represent the First Amendment interests of the publisher. The court said that a copy of the notice the prison gave to the inmate also should be sent to the publisher.[21]

Test for outgoing mail

While the Supreme Court created a new test for restricting incoming mail in the *Abbott* case, it left the test for outgoing mail unchanged because the Court felt as a general rule that outgoing mail presents substantially less of a security threat than does incoming mail. To reject a piece of outgoing mail, a stronger case must be made showing that the letter threatens security or rehabilitation and that there are no less restrictive alternative ways of responding to this threat other than refusing to mail the letter.

Facility policy should indicate the grounds for rejecting publications or letters and the procedure that should be followed in making such decisions. These policies should be followed carefully and rejection decisions carefully documented.

Legal mail

Special requirements apply to mail to inmates from attorneys, the courts, and other government officials (legal mail). Such mail may be protected by a legal privilege (as with attorney-client mail) as well as by the Constitution. Therefore, such mail normally cannot be read by institution staff and should be opened only in the presence of the inmate and examined at that point for contraband.

Media mail

Does mail between an inmate and the media (TV or radio stations, newspaper reporters, and so forth) have a special status, like legal mail? Although a 1978 case from Texas did hold that media mail was "privileged" and must be handled with the same precautions as legal mail, more recent cases have rejected that ruling and criticized it. Therefore, most courts now probably would hold that media mail is entitled to no special privileges, but may be treated as any other normal type of mail.[22]

Publishers-only rules

Rules requiring that books and other publications be sent to inmates only from publishers (publishers-only rules) have been upheld as furthering valid security concerns.[23] A publishers-only rule was seen as a preferable alternative to a jail's policy of banning all hardbound books, even when they came from a publisher. Another alternative that the court said would have been acceptable was for the institution to tear the covers off the books. But a total ban (particularly when combined with the lack of any library facilities or softbound books) was unconstitutional for an inmate held in a jail nearly 1,000 days who was seeking literature on alcoholism.[24]

Visiting

The importance of visiting in both the prison and jail setting is recognized by correctional professionals. However, the Supreme Court has refused to hold that at least due process (part of the Fourteenth Amendment) guarantees inmates an unfettered right to visits.[25]

Some lower courts have ordered that pretrial detainees be afforded the opportunity for limited amounts of visitation, but the Supreme Court has twice held that inmates do not have any right to contact visits.[26] If there is no right to contact visiting, there also obviously is no right to conjugal visiting, although a number of correctional facilities allow conjugal visiting as a matter of policy.

A developing question related to visiting is whether female inmates have a right to breast-feed their infants. The general answer is probably "no," but under somewhat unique circumstances, one court said that an institution at least had to allow a woman to breast-feed her baby in the visiting room, when the mother and child otherwise would have been together. The court noted that mothers were allowed to bottle-feed their babies during regular visits and could see no reason not to allow breast-feeding under the same circumstances. Even in this case, the court refused to require the institution to store or otherwise handle the mother's milk.[27]

Association and Group Activities

Institution officials have almost complete authority to restrict or prohibit inmate group activities. Inmates in the North Carolina prison system attempted to form a prisoners' union, hold meetings, and prepare and distribute written literature. Prison officials barred such activity even though the bar limited inmates' ability to exercise their First Amendment rights of speech and association. The Supreme Court approved the actions of the officials, noting that speech rights were barely implicated and that associational rights were curtailed "by the realities of confinement."[28] Unless the security concerns of the officials could be shown conclusively to be wrong, they should prevail.

Conclusion

While courts are more willing to side with the institution in dealing with First Amendment questions than they have been in years past, First Amendment issues remain legally sensitive. Staff should be aware of these issues when they are dealing with First Amendment issues and act with care in those areas.

Review Questions

1. What is the most common justification for restricting inmates' First Amendment rights?

2. An inmate sends a letter to his mother criticizing the warden of the prison. May the institution refuse to mail this letter? Why or why not?

3. Has the Supreme Court been increasing or decreasing the amount of deference lower courts must show to the judgment of correctional officials?

Notes

1. *Turner v. Safley*, 107 S.Ct. 2254 (1987). *O'Lone v. Estate of Shabazz*, 107 S.Ct. 2400 (1987).
2. *Africa v. Commonwealth of Pennsylvania*, 662 F.2d 1025, 1032 (3rd Cir., 1981).
3. *Patrick v. Lefevre*, 745 F.2d 153, 158 (2d Cir., 1984).
4. *U.S. v. Meyers*, 95 F.3d 1475 (10th Cir., 1996).
5. *Jackson v. Mann*, 196 F.3d 316, 320 (2d Cir., 1999).
6. *Dettmer v. Landon*, 799 F.2d 929 (4th Cir., 1986).
7. *Theriault v. A Religious Office*, 895 F.2d 104 (2d Cir., 1990). This case also cites many of the CONS decisions.

8. *Jones v. Bradley*, 590 F.2d 294 (9th Cir., 1979).
9. *Vaughn v. Garrison*, 534 F.Supp. 1111 (E.D. La., 1981). Childs v. Duckworth, 509 F.Supp. 1254 (N.D. Ind., 1981).
10. *Theriault v. Silber*, 547 F.2d 1279 (5th Cir., 1977), cert denied, 98 S.Ct. 216 (1977).
11. *Thompson v. Commonwealth of Kentucky*, 712 F.2d 1078 (6th Cir., 1983).
12. *Johnson v. Horn*, 150 F.3d 276 (3rd Cir., 1998).
13. *Udey v. Kastner*, 805 F.2d 1218 (5th Cir., 1986).
14. *Abbott v. Thornburgh*, 824 F.2d 1166 (D.C. Cir., 1987), reversed, *Thornburgh v. Abbott*, 109 S.Ct. 1874 (1989). The earlier case relied upon was *Procunier v. Martinez*, 94 S.Ct. 1800 (1974).
15. *Dawson v. Scurr*, 986 F.2d 257 (8th Cir., 1993).
16. *Hause v. Vaught*, 993 F.2d 1079 (4th Cir., 1993).
17. *Harper v. Wallingford*, 877 F.2d 728 (9th Cir., 1989).
18. *Mauro v. Arpaio*, 194 F.3d 1317 (9th Cir., 1999).
19. *Amatel v. Reno*, 156 F.3d 192 (D.C. Cir., 1998).
20. *Procunier v. Martinez,* 94 S.Ct. 1800 (1974).
21. *Montcalm Pub. Corp. v. Beck*, 80 F.3d 105 (4th Cir., 1996).
22. *Guajuardo v. Estelle*, 580 F.2d 748 (5th Cir., 1978), but see *Mann v. Adams*, 846 F.2d 591 (9th Cir., 1988), criticizing the reasoning and conclusion in *Guajuardo*, and *Gaines v. Lane*, 790 F.2d 1299 (7th Cir., 1986), also holding media mail is not privileged in any way.
23. *Bell v. Wolfish*, 441 U.S. 529 (1979).
24. *Jackson v. Elrod,* 881 F.2d 441 (7th Cir., 1989).
25. *Kentucky v. Thompson*, 109 S.Ct. 1904 (1989).
26. *Bell v. Wolfish*, 441 U.S. 520 (1979). *Block v. Rutherford,* 104 S.Ct. 3227 (1984).
27. Not required, *Sutherland v. Thigpen*, 784 F.2d 713 (5th Cir., 1986). Required during visits, *Berrios-Berrios v. Thornburgh*, 716 F.Supp. 989 (E.D. Ky, 1989).
28. *Jones v. North Carolina Prisoners' Labor Union*, 433 U.S. 119 (1977).

VII.
The Fourth Amendment:
Searches and Seizures

The Fourth Amendment provides, in part, security from unwarrantable search and seizure:

> The right of the people to be secure in their persons, houses, papers, and effects, against unreasonable searches and seizures, shall not be violated . .

In plain English, the Fourth Amendment means the government cannot conduct *unreasonable* searches or seizures. What an "unreasonable" search is varies. At one extreme, law enforcement officers usually cannot search the person or home of a member of the general public without a search warrant (a document issued by a judicial officer that grants permission for the search and verifies that the judicial officer has been convinced that "probable cause" exists to provide justification for the search). At the other extreme, corrections officials may strip search inmates returning from contact visits without a warrant and without any particular suspicion that an inmate is smuggling contraband.

The Balancing Test

Search warrants are not required for all types of searches government officials might want to make and are virtually never required for the searches that might be made in a prison or jail by the facility staff. But what determines whether a particular type of search must be based on a warrant? Or may the search be based on some level of particularized suspicion? ("*Particularized*" suspicion refers to situations where the finger of suspicion points at one individual. By contrast, a *"generalized" suspicion* focuses on a group of persons. It is the difference between suspecting that a particular inmate is carrying contraband at a specific time and suspecting that some inmates in the population are carrying contraband.) Another question is when may searches be done randomly?

As with many other areas of inmates' rights, deciding what a "reasonable" inmate search is involves a balancing test. In applying the balancing test, a court generally asks three basic questions. The first two are whether the person being searched has a subjective (personal) expectation of privacy and then whether society is prepared to recognize that expectation of privacy as reasonable. In other words, does society attach an objective expectation of privacy to the type of search conducted. If the answer to either of these questions is "no," then the person has no Fourth Amendment protections. Courts generally have held that inmates have at least some limited expectations of privacy. However, these expectations are substantially less than persons in the free community have.

Assuming the person has some reasonable expectations of privacy, then the third question arises: does the government have a strong enough reason for conducting the search to justify intruding into the reasonable expectation of privacy the person enjoys? This is where the balancing of inmate rights and institutional interests takes place. The more intrusive a search is, the greater the expectation of privacy will be and the greater the justification the government must show.

A very common example of the balancing test in action is familiar to anyone who flies in commercial airliners. As a condition of boarding the airplane, one must go through a limited search. If there were not a real concern about airline hijackings, these searches probably would be unconstitutional. But because of the government's interest in preventing hijackings, the searches are legally acceptable. However, if the government proposed subjecting all fliers to automatic strip searches, which are far more intrusive than a magnetometer search, then courts undoubtedly would rule that the government's need to prevent hijackings was not strong enough to justify such massive intrusions into the privacy of airline passengers.

In the context of a prison or jail, the court should balance the intrusion into the inmate's legitimate expectation of privacy and the institution's interest in making that intrusion using the *Turner* Test[1] (*see* Chapter V.). Remember, this test generally requires courts to give the benefit of the doubt to prison officials regarding matters of security.

Just as inmates' expectations of privacy are reduced by the fact of incarceration, the expectations of free people entering a correctional facility are reduced, although not as much as inmates.' Thus, visitors and staff are more subject to search in the facility than they would be on the street.

Case Study: Strip Searches Approved, but Not Verbal Harassment

Inmates in the segregation unit at the Iowa State Penitentiary were strip searched every time they moved in or out of the unit. All inmates were strip searched before and after contact visits. This included visits with lawyers, clergy, and the prison ombudsman and before and after going to medical facilities, court appearances, or exercise areas.

The district court entered an injunction against the lawyer and medical visit searches, since the court believed some inmates were discouraged from exercising their constitutional rights to attorney visits and medical care because of their distaste for the strip searches. The court of appeals reversed the lower court and upheld the searches, noting from testimony and other sources that inmates often attempt to smuggle contraband in body cavities and that officials had strong security concerns justifying the searches.

But the court of appeals upheld one portion of the district court's injunction. The lower court had found that some officers, in some situations, accompanied strip searches with "teasing, rude and offensive comments, and other verbal harassment." An injunction prohibiting such conduct was upheld, the court saying "[verbal harassment] is demeaning and bears no relationship to the prison's legitimate security needs." *Goff v. Nix*, 803 F.2d 358 (8th Cir., 1986).

One relatively dramatic difference between traditional law enforcement searches and searches conducted in a correctional facility is that courts uniformly recognize that search warrants are virtually never required to conduct searches of inmates. Some facilities may require a search warrant as a condition to performing a body cavity probe search, but courts generally have held that the Fourth Amendment requires only reasonable suspicion, and no warrant, for such searches. *See* the discussion of body cavity probe searches later in this chapter.

Another factor that a court may consider in deciding if a particular search is "reasonable" or not is the manner in which the search is conducted. Is the search done professionally, or is it done in a way that unnecessarily humiliates and embarrasses the person being searched?

Doing searches in a professional, nondegrading way is one of the most important things for a correctional officer to remember about legally proper searches. Unprofessional behavior can include such things as making rude, insulting, or demeaning remarks to the inmate during the search, or performing the search in a way or in a place that unnecessarily exposes the inmate to view by others not involved with the search. Doing a cell search is generally reasonable, but leaving the cell in total disarray may turn the generally reasonable search into one that is unreasonable.

"Reasonable Suspicion": What Is It?

Given that warrants are typically not required for searches of inmates, one of the major questions courts have addressed when evaluating different types of searches which take place in a correctional facility is whether a type of search can be done randomly, without any particular reason to suspect that an inmate is carrying contraband, or whether some reason exists to suspect a particular inmate may be carrying contraband. This is referred to as "particularized suspicion" and where it is necessary to justify a given category of searches, courts ask if "reasonable suspicion" existed.

Probably the most controversial and often litigated type of inmate search where reasonable suspicion is required is strip searches of persons being booked into jails. This is discussed in greater detail later in the chapter.

The phrase "reasonable suspicion" needs to be understood because it has a relatively specific meaning to a court. Reasonable suspicion (or *"reasonable belief"*) is a low level of "cause" for a search (*"probable cause"* is a somewhat higher level of cause).

1. The suspicion usually must be focused on the person to be searched. In other words, the cause must be "particularized."
2. There must be a specific fact, combined with the reasonable inferences that can be drawn from the fact in light of

experience, for reasonable suspicion to exist. (Fact + judgment = reasonable suspicion.)

Examples of reasonable suspicion cases include the following:

- Where evidence showed two officers were seen smoking next to a fence and marijuana later was smelled, there was no reasonable suspicion justifying searches of the officers.

- Where informant information was received from a person who had no prior record of providing reliable information and there was nothing else to corroborate the information, no reasonable suspicion existed.

- Where an inmate informant and other officers reported on the smuggling conduct of an officer and large amounts of contraband were entering the facility, reasonable suspicion did exist.[2] Anonymous tips alone will not create reasonable suspicion.

In general, "reasonable suspicion" searches demand that suspicion be focused on a single individual. When relying on informant tips, the informant should be reliable. And the suspicion must come from some sort of objective fact, not just a hunch. Tips from anonymous informants, without more evidence, are generally not sufficient to provide reasonable suspicion.

Because determining the existence of reasonable suspicion involves a judgment call, it is impossible to provide a written definition of reasonable suspicion that will allow the officer trying to make the determination of whether reasonable suspicion exists in a particular situation do so with total confidence.

Where any type of search, but particularly a strip or body cavity probe search, is done only after someone decides there is sufficient reason to conduct such a search (reasonable suspicion), the basis for the search should be documented. Such documentation then can provide the basis either for the agency administration to review the decision or the basis for defending the decision in court, should a lawsuit be filed. If the officer or supervisor making the decision does not document the reason, the reason may be forgotten and the search impossible to justify in court. The testimony in court in such a case might go something like this:

> **Lawyer for the plaintiff**: Sergeant Harris, did you approve strip searching my client?
>
> **Sgt. Harris**: According to the shift log, yes.
>
> **Lawyer**: Your agency's rules require a finding of reasonable suspicion as a condition to strip search someone. What was the reasonable suspicion in this case?
>
> **Sgt. Harris**: I don't remember.
>
> **Judge** (later): The law requires reasonable suspicion for this type of search. It is the institution's burden in this case to show there was reasonable suspicion. Since Sergeant Harris cannot remember why he ordered the search, I find there was no reasonable suspicion and rule for the plaintiff.

Searches in Prison and Jails

Maintaining security is basic to running a prison or jail. The threat to security caused by contraband smuggled into the facility and/or carried by inmates in the facility is obvious and well recognized by the courts. Therefore, the courts accept the compelling need for security as being justification to reduce the scope of the Fourth Amendment's protections inside the institution to far less than they are outside. But this does not mean that no protections exist. The extent of the protections that exist for inmates increases as the searches become more intrusive.

Cell searches

The Supreme Court has held that inmates simply have no expectation of privacy in their cells, and, therefore, the Fourth Amendment does not even apply to cell searches. Cell searches then may be conducted at random, without any sort of cause or suspicion needed to justify searching a particular cell.[3] The Court also has ruled that inmates have no right to be present when their cells are searched.[4]

NOTE: A type of search that courts say is "reasonable" may still be done in a way that makes the search unreasonable. Therefore, despite the lack of Fourth Amendment protections regarding cell searches,

searches that leave a cell in shambles may lead to court intervention.[5] As a general practice, cells should be left more or less as neat after a search as they were before the search.

Case Study: Body Cavity Probe Searches and Court Review

A body cavity probe search is as intrusive a search as possible, short of surgery. As such, courts will carefully and critically review the justifications for body cavity probe searches as well as the manner in which they are conducted.

The Walla Walla State Penitentiary had a policy of doing digital body cavity probe searches, including rectal probes, of every inmate who entered or returned to a super-maximum custody unit. Such a policy was, at best, on the very edge of constitutionality. In an opinion that, for procedural reasons, did not ultimately decide the merits of the case, a reviewing court tentatively decided the searches, as apparently actually carried out, were being done for punitive reasons not related to security concerns. As such, they violated the clearly established rights of the inmates. The court noted the following factors in reaching its conclusion:

1. An officer who picked up one inmate in the general population to escort him to the unit allegedly smiled and said, "Today, you meet Mr. Big Finger."
2. Although every inmate entering the unit was rectally probe-searched, no effort was apparently made to search other body cavities, hair, or even hands. Evidence showed one inmate had smuggled a pack of tobacco into the unit in his pocket.
3. The rectal probe search policy allegedly was used by officers as a threat to influence inmates' behavior in the general population. *Tribble v. Gardner*, 860 F.2d 321 (9th Cir., 1988).

Case Study: Visitor Body Cavity Probe and Search Warrant

Sometimes even a search warrant does not protect officers from liability for an unconstitutional search. Consider the following case, involving suspected drug trafficking between an inmate and his wife.

Prison officials obtained a search warrant from a local judge allowing them to perform body cavity searches of an inmate's pregnant wife and infant son. The search was conducted, but no drugs were found. The wife then filed a civil rights action against the prison investigators. Even though the local magistrate had reviewed the affidavit submitted in support of the search warrant and found it adequate, the federal court not only found the affidavit insufficient, but said that "no reasonably competent officer could have believed that the affidavit established probable cause for a body cavity search." Based on this conclusion, the court denied the defendants' qualified immunity, exposing them to liability for damages.

Defendants argued that no probable cause was necessary because the plaintiff was a prison visitor and only reasonable suspicion is required to search prison visitors. Conceding that reasonable suspicion ("specific, objective facts and rational inferences" therefrom) will support a strip search of a visitor, the court found a manual body cavity probe search, as was conducted here, to require a search warrant issued upon probable cause. The court found the defendants' argument about reasonable suspicion failed for another reason. When the wife came to the prison and was searched, prison officials were waiting for her, waiting to do the search. They had no intention of allowing her to visit. Since this was the case, the court reasoned that the woman presented no threat to prison security and her search could not be justified as furthering legitimate penological concerns. The situation had changed from one involving prison security to nothing more than a criminal investigation. *Laughter v. Kay*, 986 F.Supp. 1362 (D.Utah, 1997).

Pat down searches

The courts also generally have upheld the reasonableness of pat down searches being done randomly. Again, if it can be shown that pat downs are being done to harass particular inmates and are not being done for a legitimate institutional purpose, a court may intervene. Cross-gender pat searches may present special problems, *see* page 82.

Urine tests

Random urine tests for inmates, while seen as a form of search, have been approved by the courts. Again, the way the urine sample is obtained could be seen as unreasonable, if it exposes the inmate to unnecessary humiliation. If staff observe the inmate providing the urine sample, the staff actually doing the observation should be the same sex as the inmate. This is a good example of an objective expectation of privacy: society generally believes that persons reasonably expect they will not be observed urinating by a person of the opposite sex.

Strip searches

The Supreme Court reluctantly has approved strip searches of all inmates following their exposure to the opportunity to obtain contraband, such as after a contact visit or trip to a hospital.[6] Courts also have approved strip searching inmates when they leave segregation unit cells because of the especially great security concerns those units present.[7]

Surprisingly, there has been almost no recent litigation regarding strip searching inmates in the general population of an institution at other times. Most facilities restrict such strip searches to circumstances when there is reasonable suspicion that the inmate may be concealing contraband.

In one case, a district court approved a policy under which two cells were selected at random every day to be thoroughly searched. These searches included strip searches of the inmates housed in the cells.[8]

Agency policy should address when inmates may be strip searched. Because of the legal sensitivity of strip searches, staff should follow such policies with care. Particular attention should be paid to documenting the need for a strip search when the search is based on a discretionary decision.

Case Study: Sexual Abuse of Female Inmates

As the twenty-first century begins, one likes to think that correctional agencies run at a high level of professionalism and that the sort of shocking cases which opened the door for court intervention in corrections years ago do not arise anymore. Unfortunately, they do. Not with the frequency they once did, but consider the following:

The woman was an inmate in the District of Columbia jail in 1995. Over the course of a month, correctional officers forced her, along with other female inmates, to participate in strip shows and exotic dances. At least once, the inmates danced in the nude. Several officers were involved, but no supervisory officials apparently knew of the incidents. Eighty to one hundred women were in the units where the dancing took place, but supervisory officials apparently only became aware of the incidents when the lawsuit was filed.

One inmate testified that she refused to participate and was beaten by an officer. Defendants argued she was beaten for reasons other than refusing to dance. Another inmate testified she participated only out of fear of physical retaliation should she refuse.

Several months prior to the incidents, another federal judge had found there were substantial sexually related problems between male officers and female inmates and ordered remedial steps to be taken. When the incidents took place, all that had been done was the issuance of a new policy and limited training.

Based on these facts, the court directed a verdict in favor of the plaintiff, leaving the jury with only the task of assessing damages. *Newby v. District of Columbia*, 59 F.Supp.2d 35 (D.D.C. 1999).

Jail strip searches

There have been many lawsuits about jails strip searching arrestees at the time of their admission to the jail. Without exception, courts across the country have held that automatic strip searches of persons arrested and booked for minor offenses are unreasonable and violate the Fourth Amendment.[9] Many of these cases have resulted in substantial amounts of damages being paid to the arrestees. A jail that persists in strip searching all arrestees places itself at serious legal risk.

Courts consistently say that reasonable suspicion is required to strip search arrestees. This may be based on the conduct of the individual arrestee, which creates a suspicion the person may be concealing contraband. It also may be based on the reason for the arrest. If the person is arrested for a drug-related offense or violent offense, most courts say a strip search at the time of booking is constitutional. A felony charge alone does not necessarily create cause for a strip search, though in *Kennedy v. Los Angeles Police Department,* the Ninth Circuit found that a strip search of a person arrested on a minor property-related felony was not reasonable.[10] Only weeks earlier, the same court (but different judges) found that felony auto theft was sufficiently associated with violence to justify a strip search.[11]

Some have argued that when an arrestee is placed in the general population of a jail, a strip search may be conducted. This argument was rejected in the *Kennedy* case—placing the woman arrested for the property offense in the general population did not create justification for a strip search when none existed otherwise.

Jail staff involved with the booking process will be responsible for making the decision to strip search an arrestee. As the two cases just discussed show, the decision to strip search someone must be made very carefully. Carefully written policy should provide as much guidance as possible. Where discretionary strip searches are made, it also will be important to document the reasons for conducting these searches.

Body cavity probe searches

In extreme situations, it may be necessary to physically probe an inmate's body cavities for contraband. This is the most intrusive search of the person possible.

In a normal institutional setting, reasonable cause must exist to justify a body cavity probe search. There must be some reason to suspect a particular inmate is hiding contraband in a body cavity.[12] In extraordinarily high-security housing units, automatic probe searches done every time an inmate returns to his or her cell have been approved, but this is clearly the exception, requiring a very clear showing of need to justify.[13]

Body cavity probe searches are best done only when there is good reason to believe the inmate is carrying contraband in a body cavity (perhaps even probable cause, but certainly reasonable suspicion or belief). The search should be done by medical staff and done in a manner and place that respects the inmate's dignity and privacy as much as is reasonably possible. Facility policy should address circumstances in which body cavity probe searches may be done.

Visitor searches

Visitors are entitled to greater protections from searches than inmates, although visitors give up some of their expectations of privacy on entering the prison or jail. Routine pat downs, searches of purses and briefcases, and magnetometer searches of all persons entering a facility have been approved. But courts require reasonable suspicion for a strip search to be performed. Usually even when reasonable suspicion exists, the person may refuse to submit to the search and leave the institution.

A requirement that every visitor "agree" to a strip search as a condition of being allowed to visit jail inmates resulted in an award of $177,000 damages against a Massachusetts sheriff.[14] The court quickly rejected the argument that the visitor "consented" to the searches, saying that at least as a general matter, the state cannot condition the granting of even a privilege (such as visiting) on someone giving up a constitutional right (in this case, the right to be free from unreasonable searches).

Just as reasonable suspicion is required for visitor strip searches, so is it required for staff strip searches. Thus, an anonymous tip did not justify strip searching an officer, since it could not provide reasonable suspicion.[15]

Observation and Searches by the Opposite Sex

The increased use of women working in male facilities and, to a lesser extent, men working in female facilities, presents a variety of issues, many arising under the Fourth Amendment.

Does it violate the right of privacy of the inmate (which comes in part from the Fourth Amendment) if the inmate is observed taking a shower, using the toilet, or in other states of undress by an officer of the opposite sex? Does it make a difference if the officer is a woman and the inmate male or if the inmate is a woman and the officer male? Can officers search inmates of the opposite sex? If a cross-gender pat down search is acceptable, is a strip search? Does the guarantee of equal employment opportunity outweigh privacy rights the inmate might have regarding being observed (or touched) by an officer of the opposite sex? Not all of these questions have been answered yet, but some answers are emerging.

Female officers in male units

In *Dothard v. Rawlinson*, the Supreme Court decided that a complete ban on women working in a male prison system did not violate the equal opportunity rights of the women. This decision was not based on inmate privacy concerns, but instead on a concern for the women's safety, in light of the "jungle-like" conditions in the prison.[16] This decision has not been followed by later courts, but instead is limited to its facts. To argue that the *Dothard* case justified an all-male workforce, one virtually would concede conditions in the facility were so unsafe as to be unconstitutional.

The trend now is to hold that when female officers only casually or incidentally observe male inmates in states of undress, it does not violate any rights of the inmates. While some early cases in this area tried to require the institution to accommodate the privacy interests of the inmate through such methods as erecting privacy screens or juggling staff schedules, the trend today is to tolerate limited glimpses of nudity.[17]

Male officers in female facilities

The only major court decision in several years dealing with men working in women's facilities tentatively approved almost a complete ban on men working in housing units, not because of an invasion of privacy, but because the institution warden suggested the female inmates' rehabilitation would be enhanced by a relatively male-free environment, since a high percentage of the women had been physically or sexually abused by men.[18] The suit was not filed by inmates but by male officers, who claimed the ban violated their rights against sexual discrimination in the workplace.

Sexual abuse of female inmates by male officers has been a serious problem in a number of jurisdictions.[19] This abuse ranges from verbal harassment to unwarranted intrusions in women's privacy, to unwarranted touching to physical rape. This conduct may violate the Fourth Amendment, the Eighth Amendment (cruel and unusual punishment), or even may be considered criminal behavior exposing the officer to prosecution. Many states have made any sexual contact between a correctional officer and an inmate a crime.

Typically, "consent" is not a relevant consideration: *any* sexual contact, regardless of supposed consent, violates the law. Sexual contact between officer and inmate under any circumstances is completely inappropriate, if not illegal. While most of the controversy over officer-inmate sexual contact relates to male officers and female inmates, improper contact between female officers and male inmates also occurs. Undoubtedly, sexual contact between officers and inmates of the same sex also takes place. In all cases, the contact is entirely inappropriate.

Cross-gender pat searches

Some courts have approved pat searches of male inmates by female officers, while others have done so under the assumption that the searches did not include contact with the genital area.[20] So, it is not totally clear that female officers may pat search male inmates.

While courts may be willing to allow female officers to pat search male inmates, the same cannot be said of male officers pat searching female inmates. This practice has been addressed only once by a federal appeals court, and the court held that the practice was cruel and unusual punishment, in violation of the Eighth Amendment. The court refused to evaluate the searches under the Fourth Amendment. In deciding the searches violated the Eighth Amendment, the court was reacting to expert testimony that said that many of the women, who had been sexually and physically abused prior to coming into prison, would be psychologically traumatized by being pat searched by male officers, since they would see this as a continuation of the abuse they had previously suffered.[21]

In the three years following the *Jordan* decision, no other court outside the Ninth Circuit has addressed a similar question of male officers pat searching female inmates. *Jordan* did not address the question of female officers pat searching male inmates.

A good deal more litigation will be needed before there are complete, clear answers to the legal questions surrounding cross-gender supervision, although the legal trend at this time certainly favors women at least working in an increasing number of posts in male facilities. Something that makes this area even more difficult to analyze than many other "inmate rights" areas is that it involves conflicts between interests of the inmate and the institution (a common situation) and interests of the officers in equal opportunity and avoiding discrimination.

Where a task requires fairly intensive observation of naked inmates (such as doing strip searches), the task only should be done by persons of the same sex. In emergency situations, considerations of privacy in searches generally are set aside in favor of the institution being able to respond to the emergency in the quickest, safest, most effective way.

Conclusion

The rights of inmates to be free from unreasonable searches is drastically less than the right enjoyed by persons outside the institution. But some protections remain. For the line officer asked to perform searches, the key factors to remember are to follow policy regarding when searches may be performed and to do those searches in a professional manner that respects the dignity of the inmate.

Review Questions

1 The Supreme Court has held that inmates have no expectation of privacy in regard to their cells. How then might a cell search trigger court intervention?

2. What is necessary to justify visitor strip searches?

3. What is the most important thing for correctional officers to remember when performing inmate searches?

Notes

1. *Covino v. Patrissi*, 967 F.2d 73 (2d Cir., 1992).
2. *Kennedy v. Hardiman*, 684 F.Supp. 540 (N.D. Ill., 1980).
3. *Hudson v. Palmer*, 104 S.Ct. 3194 (1984).
4. *Block v. Rutherford*, 104 S.Ct. 3227 (1984).
5. *Brown v. Hilton*, 492 F.Supp. 771 (D. N.J., 1980).
6. *Bell v. Wolfish*, 441 U.S. 529 (1979).
7. *Rickman v. Avanti*, 854 F.2d 327 (9th Cir., 1988), *Goff v. Nix*, 803 F.2d 358 (8th Cir., 1986), cert. denied, 108 S.Ct. 115 (1987).
8. *Covino v. Patrissi,* 967 F.2d 73 (2d Cir., 1992).
9. In *Chapman v. Nichols*, 989 F.2d 393 (10th Cir., 1993), the court cites opinions from eight different federal appeals courts holding that strip searching arrestees without reasonable suspicion is a violation of the Fourth Amendment.
10. *Kennedy v. Los Angeles Police Department*, 887 F.2d 920 (9th Cir., 1989).
11. *Thompson v. Los Angeles* (County), 885 F.2d 1439 (9th Cir., 1989).
12. *Vaughn v. Ricketts*, 663 F.Supp. 410 (D. Ariz., 1987).
13. *Bruscino v. Carlson*, 854 F.2d 162 (7th Cir., 1988).
14. *Blackburn v. Snow*, 771 F.2d 556 (1st Cir., 1985).
15. *Security and Law Enforcement Employees District Council #82 v. Carey,* 737 F.2d 187 (2d Cir., 1984).
16. *Dothard v. Rawlinson*, 433 U.S. 321 (1977).
17. *Michenfelder v. Sumner*, 860 F.2d 328 (9th Cir., 1988). *Hardin v. Stynchcomb*, 691 F.2d 1364 (11th Cir., 1982), *Timm v. Gunter*, 917 F.2d 1093 (8th Cir., 1990).
18. *Torres v. Wisconsin Department of Health and Social Services*, 859 F.2d 1523 (7th Cir., 1988).
19. Women's Rights Project of Human Rights Watch. 1996. *All Too Familiar Sexual Abuse of Women in U.S. State Prisons.* New York.
20. *Grummett v. Rushen*, 779 F.2d 491 (9th Cir., 1985). *Smith v. Fairman*, 678 F.2d 52 (7th Cir., 1982).
21. *Jordan v. Gardner*, 986 F.2d 1521 (9th Cir., 1993).

VIII.
The Eighth Amendment: Cruel and Unusual Punishment

The Eighth Amendment addresses bails, fines, and punishments:

> Excessive bail shall not be required, nor excessive fines imposed, nor cruel and unusual punishment inflicted.

Through its "cruel and unusual punishment" clause, the Eighth Amendment has been more significant for corrections than any other amendment during the inmate rights movement. It is through the concept of cruel and unusual punishment that conditions of confinement in a jail, prison, or even an entire prison system may be challenged.

The Eighth Amendment also may provide claims of the use of excess force (*see* Chapter10) as well as the basis for suits challenging such things as the adequacy of medical care or protection afforded an inmate in particular situations. Offenders also may use the cruel and unusual punishment clause to challenge the length or severity of their sentences (especially in death penalty cases), but this aspect of the amendment is not usually of direct concern to correctional officers, nor are claims relating to excessive bail or fines.

Unlike most other amendments where one may compare what the amendment means, or its scope, between noncustodial situations ("the street") and inside the institution, the Eighth Amendment has no "street" application. Cruel and unusual punishment applies only after an offender has been convicted. Eighth Amendment rights arise or are created by the fact of conviction.

A Vague Concept

The phrase "cruel and unusual punishment" is vague, making it difficult to define in concrete terms. What may be cruel and unusual punishment to one observer may be standard operating procedure to another. The courts have tried to develop other, clearer ways of defining the concept, but these are also vague phrases that may mean different things to different people. Among the phrases or "tests" the Supreme Court has developed over the years to define or clarify what cruel and unusual punishment means are the following:

- shocks the conscience of the Court
- violates the evolving standards of decency of a civilized society
- punishment that is disproportionate to the offense
- involves the wanton and unnecessary infliction of pain

Some types of punishment, such as flogging or other forms of physical torture, uniformly would be seen as being cruel and unusual punishment. But with many conditions and practices, it is not clear if they are or are not cruel and unusual punishment. Because the concept of cruel and unusual punishment never will have a clear, objective definition that means the same thing to different people, it is virtually impossible to look at every imaginable situation and say with confidence, "This is (or is not) cruel and unusual punishment."

During the early 1990s, the courts seem to have settled on the "wanton and unnecessary infliction of pain" test, with the Supreme Court applying this test in cases involving conditions of confinement and the use of force.[1]

Except for use of force claims, most Eighth Amendment issues inmates raise require the court to examine the state of mind of the defendants as part of deciding if the inmate has received cruel and unusual punishment. The defendant must have shown "deliberate indifference" to some significant basic human need of the inmate, such as medical care.

The phrase "deliberate indifference" first appeared in a Supreme Court case in 1976 in the case of *Estelle v. Gamble*.[2] There, the Court said that deliberate indifference to an inmate's serious medical need violated the Eighth Amendment. State of mind questions also are relevant in failure to protect cases, in conditions of confinement cases, and in other cases where an inmate complains that some basic human need is not being met adequately.

Although the concept of deliberate indifference has been part of Eighth Amendment litigation for many years, it was not until 1994 that the Court defined the phrase. In a failure to protect case, where a transsexual inmate was raped after being placed in the general population of a federal penitentiary, the Court said that to be deliberately indifferent, an official must have actual knowledge that an inmate faces a substantial risk of serious harm and then must disregard that risk by failing to take reasonable steps to abate it.[3] In *Farmer*, it was not clear from the record what the defendants (all at the level of warden or above) actually knew about the inmate's circumstances, so the case was sent back to the lower courts for trial. Ironically, when the case was finally tried, the jury found that the plaintiff failed to prove he even had been sexually assaulted. Therefore, the jury did not have to consider whether the defendants had been deliberately indifferent to the inmate's safety.

Conditions of Confinement

Conditions of confinement cases, often referred to as overcrowding cases, have resulted in one or more prisons in almost every state being found to be unconstitutional at one time or another. As of September 30, 1999, twenty-five states plus the District of Columbia, Puerto Rico, and the Virgin Islands were under court order or consent decrees to limit their prison populations and/or to improve conditions in one or more prisons. In seven states, the entire prison system was under court order. Only two states, Minnesota and North Dakota never have been involved in an overcrowding or conditions lawsuit.[4] Hundreds of jails have been under similar orders over the years.[5]

Whatever the precise numbers are, it safely can be said that a large number of America's prisons and jails have been affected directly by conditions of confinement lawsuits. And virtually every other facility in the country, new or old, has been indirectly affected by these suits.

Conditions cases are very complex and may take a long time to prepare for trial. The trial itself may continue for weeks or even months. But the time consumed in preparing and trying a conditions case is short compared to the time it often takes to correct problems when a facility is found to violate the Eighth Amendment.

NOTE: While the Eighth Amendment is the legal vehicle used to attack conditions in prisons, its protections do not apply to persons who have not yet been convicted of a crime. Since *Bell v. Wolfish*, the Due Process Clause of the Fourteenth Amendment is the vehicle used to challenge conditions of pretrial detainees. Despite the differing legal theories used for convicted versus unconvicted persons, the end result for either a prison or a jail in terms of what conditions are required is essentially the same.

Issues in conditions cases

What are the issues in conditions cases? What factors are of concern to the court? The factors courts have considered in evaluating the conditions of confinement have changed somewhat over the years. Many early cases reacted to the "totality of conditions." Under this approach, virtually all of the negative aspects of a prison would be lumped together for consideration by the court. This could be a very subjective way of analyzing conditions. Along with the totality of conditions approach, courts in the late 1970s began to focus heavily on crowding and a facility's design capacity. Under this method, several courts virtually had reached the point of deciding that if a facility held more inmates than it was designed to hold, it was in an unconstitutional state.

The Supreme Court first addressed conditions in the case of *Bell v. Wolfish*, where it held that there was "no one-man, one-cell principle lurking" in the Constitution, at least as far as pretrial detainees were concerned. Bell said that the effects of crowding on the inmates, not simply the fact of crowding, were what courts should evaluate in conditions cases. The Court reemphasized this point two years later in a case that dealt with sentenced offenders, *Rhodes v. Chapman*.[6] Conditions that are restrictive, or even harsh, do not violate the Eighth Amendment, said Justice Powell in his majority opinion. Only when conditions "deprive inmates of the minimal civilized measure of life's necessities" do they violate the Constitution, said the Court. *Bell* and *Rhodes* ended any thought that a crowded institution was *per se* unconstitutional.

Ten years passed before the Supreme Court again decided a conditions of confinement case. In *Wilson v. Seiter*,[7] the court added a new factor that must be shown in order for an institution to violate the Eighth Amendment: the inmates must prove the defendants (the persons responsible for operating the institution) were "deliberately indifferent" to conditions that denied inmates "the minimal civilized measure of life's necessities."

So, after *Wilson*, there are two separate factors that must be shown. Unless the plaintiffs (the inmates) prove both of these factors, they cannot win their case. The factors are as follows:

1. The conditions must be very bad, failing to adequately provide inmates with one or more basic human need, and
2. The defendants knew of the serious problems and failed to take any sort of meaningful corrective response (deliberate indifference).

The *Wilson* decision also said that a totality of conditions approach was incorrect. Different conditions (such as poor medical care, poor sanitation, high levels of violence) must be considered separately from one another except "when they have a mutually enforcing effect that produces the deprivation of a single, identifiable human need such as food, warmth, or exercise—for example, a low cell temperature at night combined with a failure to issue blankets."

The conditions that are the focus of the first part of the *Wilson* test will be ones that deal with the basic human needs of the inmates. These include the following:

1. **Food.** Do inmates receive a nutritionally adequate diet, and is food prepared and served in an acceptably sanitary manner?
2. **Clothing.** Does the clothing provide adequate protection given the climatic conditions, and does it provide adequate privacy protections for the inmates (is it full of holes, ragged, and so forth)? Clothing is rarely a significant issue in conditions cases anymore.
3. **Shelter.** This category looks at the overall environment of the institution, including such things as noise levels; heating; cooling; ventilation; lighting; plumbing and water supplies; overall conditions of the building; maintenance; cell size; exercise and other activity areas and opportunities, and so forth. Shelter issues often arise in cases involving old facilities.
4. **Sanitation.** This relates closely to both food and shelter. Does the plumbing leak badly? Is the institution infested with vermin? Is the facility dirty? Are proper food preparation and handling practices followed? In short, is sanitation so bad as to be

a threat to the health of the inmates? While many problems in a conditions case may be beyond the power of the line officer, sanitation is one area where institution staff can do a lot simply by insisting that the inmates keep their living units and activity areas clean and making sure that sufficient cleaning supplies are available to allow this to be done.

5. **Medical care**. Medical care is often the subject of a separate lawsuit that focuses just on the medical service delivery system. The question in either situation will be whether the medical system is so deficient as to show "deliberate indifference to the serious medical needs" of the inmates.

   While issues in the medical area can become quite complex and technical, the fundamental questions in evaluating the adequacy of a medical system are these: Can inmates (1) get prompt, timely access to properly trained and qualified medical professionals, (2) receive generally appropriate diagnoses of medical problems, and (3) receive timely and appropriate treatment at least for "serious" medical needs? "Medical care" includes dental and mental health care.

6. **Personal safety**. Are inmates reasonably safe in the institution, or is there a serious risk of assault, rape, or other serious injury from other inmates? The adequacy of classification systems often is at issue here: Does the facility have a functional way of separating types of inmates from one another so as to provide adequate protection? In evaluating safety issues, a court often will look at such things as violence levels and rates and requests for protective custody. Personal safety (or, if seen from the other side of the issue, violence levels in the institution) is often the most serious issue in crowding cases, where the sheer number of inmates may make it virtually impossible to maintain an adequate level of safety.

7. **Exercise**. In relatively extreme situations, the lack of exercise may amount to cruel and unusual punishment. Lack of exercise generally only becomes an issue in maximum-security units where inmates may be locked down without any exercise for extended periods of time.

Crowding is not a direct concern of the court in deciding whether conditions in an institution violate the Constitution. But, at the same time, crowding is probably now the single most important factor in conditions cases because as a facility becomes more and more crowded, the systems it has in place to provide basic human needs to inmates becomes overloaded and breaks down. For instance, crowding can overload the classification system, resulting in inmates not being properly separated from one another, and, in turn, contributing to an increase in violence in the institution. Other factors that also are important include the age and physical condition of the institution, the training and supervising of the officers, and the overall quality of management.

Case Study: Failure to Keep Promises Contributes to Big Contempt Fine

By agreement in 1982, the defendants agreed to the entry of a consent decree, which included a 594-inmate cap on the jail as well as other commitments about the jail. Six years later, the cap still had not been met. A second consent decree was entered into in 1987, agreeing to essentially the same things, but on a different schedule. A third agreement was entered in 1988, which included a provision for fining the defendants $100 per day per inmate over the cap if the cap was not met.

The defendants failed to meet the time limits in the decrees, even though they had agreed to them. Various hearings were held, all showing the defendants' noncompliance. After hearings in 1989, the district court imposed fines totaling more than $3.4 million, a figure that was actually reduced from what two court masters recommended. The court also ordered that the fine monies be used in part for a bail fund.

Among other comments, the judge noted ". . . the County defendants . . . have not yet spent a single dime towards alleviating the critical housing problem. [The County defendants] made the promises; they did not keep them." *Essex County Jail Inmates v. Amato*, 726 F.Supp. 539 (D. N.J., 1989).

Case Study: Harsh Conditions Not Unconstitutional for Worst of the Bad

Denying an inmate outdoor exercise for most of five years, forcing him to shower in restraints, removing his clothing at times, feeding him "nutraloaf" instead of a regular diet, placing him in constantly lit "quiet cells" are cruel and unusual punishment in some situations, perhaps, but not in the case of an inmate named Samuel LeMaire.

Mr. LeMaire was the worst of the bad in the Oregon state prison system. Serving a "life without possibility of parole" sentence, he built up what the court called an "egregious" record of the most serious types of rule violations. He attacked a sergeant and later threatened to kill him. He stabbed an inmate he thought was a snitch. He tried to stab two other officers. He routinely threw feces and urine on officers. As a result of his behavior, Mr. LeMaire spent most of five years in segregation where officials imposed the conditions he complained of from time to time. The officials carefully documented LeMaire's behavior and their attempts to respond to it in less dramatic ways. There was nothing in the record to suggest officials acted unprofessionally toward LeMaire, despite obvious provocation.

The court of appeals said that LeMaire was "the master of his own fate" and that the officials were justified in taking the steps they did. Given the extraordinary nature of LeMaire's actions, the court said that only if the record showed officials to be acting maliciously and sadistically, rather than attempting to maintain order, security, and discipline, would they violate LeMaire's rights. *LeMaire v. Maass,* 12 F.3d 1444 (9th Cir., 1993).

In other circumstances, a court might have intervened in response to these sorts of conditions. However, the documentation by Oregon officials demonstrated the appropriateness of their actions.

While a court cannot hold a facility unconstitutional simply because it is crowded, if the court decides that crowding was a primary cause of the facility being unconstitutional (such as having excessively high levels of violence), it can require the population of the facility to be lowered as part of the relief it orders.

Most conditions/crowding cases examine circumstances in an entire institution. However, sometimes the cases are more focused, and scrutinize conditions in specialized living units such as segregation, protective custody, or death row. The basic factual and legal questions in such cases are the same as in a "normal" conditions case.

Relief in Conditions Cases

Lawsuits for damages may be effectively over shortly after trial (or appeal). If damages are awarded and paid, the case is over. But conditions cases typically do not ask for damages. They ask the court to order the defendants to correct the problems that caused the facility to be unconstitutional. If the court enters such an order (*an injunction*) or if the defendants agree to such an order being entered against them (*a consent decree*), the court will continue to monitor what the defendants do until the institution or system complies with the order. This is known as the *relief phase* of the suit.

Since conditions in many facilities may be very poor or the relief requirements so complex, it often has taken years for the defendants to improve conditions to the point where the court will agree that the case may be closed. It is not uncommon for conditions cases to remain open and active for ten-to-fifteen years. For example, the entire Texas Department of Criminal Justice came under court order in a massive conditions case in 1978 at a time when the Department consisted of nearly thirty institutions and about 40,000 inmates. Defendants attempted to have the case dismissed in 1999 under the Prison Litigation Reform Act. The court grudgingly found that parts of the system met minimum constitutional requirements but that others did not, so the motion to terminate was granted in part and denied in part. After more than twenty years, the case goes on.

As institution populations surge upward, a facility trying to work itself out from under a court order based largely on crowding problems may find itself literally going backward as the population continues to grow faster than inmates can be released or new facilities constructed to hold them.

The Courts' Traditional Approach to Relief

Historically, it was not the courts' decision finding conditions violated the Eighth Amendment which created the controversy about court intervention in the operation of prisons or jails. The source of the controversy usually arose over what the court ordered defendants to do to correct the problems that created the constitutional violations. The effects of the relief a court order could extend from the institution, which was the subject of the lawsuit, to an entire department, and to an entire criminal justice system. For instance, the population cap imposed in the Texas case (referred to earlier) caused serious crowding problems (and related lawsuits) in jails across Texas because the Department could not accept convicted felons from local jails as fast as they became available. Struggling with a population cap in a local jail could affect police arrest practices, charging policies of prosecutors, and judges' decisions regarding bail and sentencing.

Where a court order addressed operational conditions (as opposed to just population levels), it became common for courts to appoint persons to oversee compliance, which often was a very detailed court order. (Defendants often settled cases through consent decrees in which the defendants voluntarily agreed to comply with rigid, detailed requirements and further agreed to the appointment of a monitor.) These persons were given different titles, different responsibilities, and differing levels of power over the defendants. The generic term used to describe them is "special master."

Traditionally, the court's relief power in this type of case is broad and very strong. While court orders typically would begin in a way the court felt was minimally intrusive, the court had the power to require defendants to address all of the underlying causes of constitutional problems. Therefore, in cases where the problems were very complex, and/or where the defendants did not appear capable of correcting problems without very active oversight, the court might enter a much more detailed, demanding order. In cases where problems appeared to be the result of crowding, these orders often took the form of population caps.

In rare, extreme situations, judges have ordered facilities closed when constitutional violations were very serious and apparently never-ending.[8] In addition to entering more demanding court orders in response to defendants' continuing failure to correct constitutional problems, courts also have exercised their traditional contempt of court powers and imposed fines on defendants. In a long-running case involving prison conditions in Puerto Rico, fines imposed on defendants (and actually paid) exceeded 200 million dollars! And as the twenty-first century begins, the case seems likely to continue for several years to come.[9]

A court usually would retain jurisdiction over a facility found unconstitutional until the requirements of the court's orders were met and it appeared that circumstances were such that if the court relinquished its oversight, the problems were not likely to return. Especially in consent decrees, where defendants had agreed in fact to do more than the Constitution might actually require, the court would continue its oversight until the requirements of the decree were met.

The Prison Litigation Reform Act and Relief

In passing the Prison Litigation Reform Act in 1996, Congress attempted to check the power of the federal courts in conditions cases. The Act begins by reinforcing the principle that injunctions in prison cases should go no further than is minimally necessary to correct constitutional violations. Population caps should be imposed only after other methods of correcting problems have been tried and failed. A single judge is prohibited from entering a population cap, which may be imposed only by a specially convened three-judge court.

Terminating injunctive orders becomes much easier under PLRA. Two years after such an order is entered, defendants may ask that it be terminated. This motion must be granted unless the court finds that some form of continuing injunctive order is needed to correct a continuing violation of a federal right. In other words, there virtually may have to be a new trial to justify continuing relief.

Special provisions exist for terminating existing consent decrees and other injunctive orders. The very detailed consent decree, which often included requirements beyond minimal demands of the Constitution, virtually is forbidden.

The powers of special masters are restricted to assisting in the development of remedial plans, holding hearings, and making proposed findings of fact. Levels of compensation for masters are fixed in the Act and now must be paid by the federal court. Defendants no longer may be required to pay costs related to a master, which in some cases in the past have amounted to hundreds of thousands of dollars.

Courts generally have upheld the major provisions of the Prison Litigation Reform Act against constitutional attack.

The Supreme Court's decision in *Lewis v. Casey*[10] strongly affirmed the High Court's belief that lower courts should proceed conservatively in ordering relief.

Alternatives to Lawsuits?

Conditions of confinement lawsuits have generated a great deal of controversy. Administrators have chafed at what they perceived (rightly so, in at least some cases) as excessive oversight from courts and masters. State and local politicians have complained about unelected federal officials in effect setting spending and criminal justice policy priorities for them. Some members of the public believe courts are responsible for creating "country club" prisons.

Case Study: Institution Does Not Guarantee Safety

An inmate was stabbed by two other inmates. The victim filed a suit against several institution officials. The evidence showed that in the weeks preceding the stabbing, officials had received two anonymous calls saying the plaintiff was in danger. In each case, officials had spoken to the inmate, who told them he knew of nothing unusual. Therefore, he was not placed in protective custody, but instead remained in the general population. Were the officials liable for a failure to protect? No. The court said that under a "deliberate indifference" standard, it was not enough to show officials were negligent. The evidence must show officials acted recklessly, that they disregarded a substantial, known risk, and that there was a strong likelihood, not simply a possibility, of injury to the inmate. Under the facts here, no such recklessness was shown. *Lewis El v. O'Leary*, 631 F.Supp. 60 (N.D. Ill., 1986).

But court intervention usually begins for a reason: an institution has very serious operational problems, perhaps the result of crowding, perhaps the result of other causes, including poor management. The problems are creating serious threats to the health or safety of inmates (and staff, although this is not an issue in the cases). Crowding may be so bad that inmates are sleeping on the floors of cells with their head almost under the toilet. Staff largely may have abandoned any efforts to keep inmates safe from one another. Where court intervention is the most dramatic, one often will find that officials have failed to correct problems which a court found to violate the rights of the inmates. The scope of the intervention has grown largely in proportion to officials' inability or refusal to address major problems seriously.

Defendants in many cases, while grumbling at times about court oversight, also will admit that without the lawsuit and without the court's orders, necessary improvements never would have been made. Instead, problems would have continued to get worse, increasing risks to both staff and inmates alike. Correctional officials may have been trying to address problems but lacked the power and the resources to solve them. Wardens and jail commanders do not determine how long inmates stay in custody. They do not appropriate the funds to increase staffing, or improve medical care. It may be that only through litigation and court intervention that the officials who do hold the keys and the purse strings can be made to focus attention on correcting very serious deficiencies. Therefore, as controversial as court intervention some-times may be, in many cases, a lawsuit or the serious threat of one may be the only effective protection against conditions deteriorating to truly unacceptable levels.

More than one correctional administrator has chosen not to invoke the provisions of the Prison Litigation Reform Act, which would allow termination of existing court orders or consent decrees because of the protections the court order provides.

Individual Eighth Amendment Issues

Eighth Amendment claims involving conditions of confinement and many inmates in a class action suit draw a great deal of attention. But Eighth Amendment issues also can arise around a single inmate. Virtually any of the issues, which can be raised in a class action Eighth

Amendment case, can be asserted by one inmate. Two types of these issues deserve special comment: medical care and failure to protect.

Medical Care

Where medical care (or the lack thereof) shows "deliberate indifference to serious medical needs," an Eighth Amendment violation exists. Medical staff can violate the Eighth Amendment. In one case, an inmate lost a large portion of his ear in a fight. He asked the doctor to sew the ear back on, but the doctor's response was to refuse the request and throw the ear in a wastebasket as the inmate watched.[11] This illustrates deliberate indifference to a serious medical need.

Other refusals by medical staff to treat inmates can create liability. The refusal by a physician's assistant to approve an X-ray for an inmate complaining of a hip injury after jumping off a truck led to a $500,000 judgment when the inmate—after only a few months in jail—had to have a total hip replacement as a result of the refusal to make any serious attempt to diagnose and treat the inmate's complaints. (The physician's assistant even refused an offer from the inmate's mother to pay for the X-ray.)[12]

Nonmedical staff also can violate the Eighth Amendment in the medical area when they impede an inmate's access to medical staff or the inmate's access to treatment, once it has been prescribed. This could involve custody staff refusing to process an inmate's request to see medical staff or refusing to allow the inmate to have crutches prescribed by a doctor because they were seen as a security threat.

Security concerns sometimes conflict with medical needs. Ignoring medical concerns for security reasons often can lead to liability. The following example is typical. An inmate is seen for an arm injury by institution medical staff, who decide the inmate needs to be transported to a local hospital for additional treatment. The doctor orders the inmate to be transported and that the inmate's arm be kept elevated during the transport. Without checking with anyone in the medical department, the transportation lieutenant overrides the "arm elevated" order because institution policy says all inmates transported outside the institution must be put in shackles and waist chains. The lieutenant's decision probably would be seen as "deliberate indifference." If the arm injury were serious and aggravated by not being kept elevated, the lieutenant could be liable.

Failure to respond to medical emergencies can create liability. Jail staff left a sixty-two-year-old in a living area where temperatures reached 110 degrees with no ventilation and extraordinarily high humidity, even though a nurse had recommended the inmate be moved. The sheriff had warned that people could die in the heat, but the county commission had done nothing to relieve the conditions because of a lack of money. There was not even a fan in the unit. The inmate passed out and, although jail staff were immediately aware of this, the inmate was given no first aid and was not taken to an emergency room for two hours. Diagnosed as suffering from heatstroke, the inmate died a few days later.[13]

The conditions in the cell, known to the sheriff and the county commission, were found to be cruel and unusual. A lack of any medical treatment from the officers showed deliberate indifference. These factors, combined with the inadequate emergency response, led to a $100,000 compensatory damage award to the victim's children and a $10,000 punitive damage award. An attorneys' fees award, probably approaching the size of the damage award, also was given. Despite all of the other heat problems, had there been a prompt emergency response that saved the inmate's life, the suit never might have been brought. Certainly, the damages would have been far lower.

This case provides an example of how "rights" to things that seem like luxuries may develop; in this case, it was a right to air conditioning. Looked at in isolation, the "right to air conditioning" seems extreme. But, suppose the case had asked for some sort of injunctive relief, instead of just asking for damages.

The court finds that the defendants were deliberately indifferent to the health needs of at least one inmate, and perhaps all the inmates, because they did nothing to relieve the extreme temperature and humidity conditions that caused one inmate to suffer a heatstroke. Having found the temperature and humidity conditions to be unconstitutional, the court asks itself: "What relief should we order that would cure this constitutional problem (excessive, health-threatening heat and humidity in the jail)?" One obvious answer is air conditioning. So, the court enters an order requiring the jail to provide air conditioning. Other persons read this order and begin to decide air conditioning must be required in jails. Other cases, also reacting to the facts, order air conditioning, and soon the "right to air conditioning" has become well established. On closer examination, the right may not be to air conditioning, but instead to "temperatures that are not so high or so low as to endanger the health of the inmates." But, in some climates, the only way this can be done is through air conditioning.

A common potential problem area for custody staff with medical care arises late at night, when an inmate suddenly says he or she needs to see a doctor. The custody staff member who tells that inmate to "wait until sick call tomorrow" in fact is making a medical decision that whatever ailment the inmate has is not serious enough to warrant immediate attention. Should a serious medical problem develop before sick call (such as appendicitis), the custody staff member could be liable. If the "wait until tomorrow" response is proper under agency policy, the agency also would be liable. Correctional facilities should develop a means by which the late-night call for medical attention can be responded to by medical staff (if even by telephone), not left to the judgment of custody staff who are not trained to make medical decisions.

Smoking

Prisons and jails have not been immune from the public controversy around smoking and exposure to secondhand smoke. Whereas not so many years ago correctional agencies might defend their policies of providing free tobacco products to inmates, now the issue is more likely to be whether the institution can go smoke-free or even whether it must provide a smoke-free environment.

Courts have denied inmate claims that they had a constitutionally protected right to smoke, thus approving smoke-free institutions.[14] The shift to smoke-free institutions is probably larger in jails than prisons. Numerous jails around the country, from very small through huge, mega-jail systems, have stopped all smoking. Contrary to fears that going smoke-free would provoke disturbances, most report the transition went smoothly and that the result is a substantial improvement. Among other benefits is a reduction in the number of fires inmates set, since they no longer have any reason for having matches. Some jail administrators note that perhaps their main problem with the smoke-free facility is the smuggling of cigarettes to inmates by officers.

In mid-1993, the Supreme Court decided that under extreme circumstances, exposing an inmate to secondhand cigarette smoke could violate the Eighth Amendment by posing an "unreasonable risk of serious damage to (the inmate's) future health."[15] The court clearly did not say that inmates have a right to a smoke-free environment. Only if the inmate could show the exposure was so serious as to create a risk that is "one that today's society chooses not to tolerate" and that prison officials were deliberately indifferent to the condition would an Eighth Amendment violation be proven. This will not be an easy burden for an inmate to meet.

The Supreme Court's smoking case is more important for addressing when risk of harm might violate the Eighth Amendment than for its specifics regarding smoking. The general principle which the case recognizes is that where there is an unreasonable risk of serious harm to inmates coming from a condition in the institution, the Eighth Amendment may be violated. Stated bluntly, this means that prison officials cannot expect to defend poor conditions or practices by arguing that "nobody is dead yet" as a result of the conditions.

Tort suits

In addition to violating the Eighth Amendment, inadequate medical care also can be the basis of a tort suit, in which it would be alleged that the care given was negligent. These cases would be brought in state court, not federal court. Showing "deliberate indifference" is legally more difficult than showing mere negligence, so tort actions about medical care may be easier for the inmate to win than civil rights suits alleging a violation of the Eighth Amendment.

Failure to Protect

While the institution does not guarantee an inmate's safety, deliberate indifference to the inmate's safety violates the Eighth Amendment. (Negligently failing to protect the inmate also may be a tort.) So, while the institution does not guarantee an inmate's safety, it (and institution staff) does have a duty to protect inmates from one another and to maintain generally acceptable levels of safety. As with medical suits, failure-to-protect suits can challenge either actions (or failures to take actions) by individual officers or can challenge the safety in an entire facility.

An Eighth Amendment violation was found under the following facts, which led the jury to award both compensatory and punitive damages to the inmate: An inmate asked not to be put in the general

101

population in the prison after coming to the institution from administrative segregation in a local jail. The request was denied. Later, a knife was found in the inmate's cell. He claimed it was "for protection" and again requested protective custody. The request was denied. Two months later, the inmate was assaulted and again asked to be removed from his cell mate. The request was denied. The cell partner later instigated a fight between the inmate and another inmate. The cell partner testified that he told a staff member to get the inmate off the floor (out of the unit). An officer with authority to move the inmate was shown to be aware of these requests and warnings. The officer was liable.[16]

Facilitywide failure-to-protect suits are one of the most common by-products of serious crowding, where simply the number of inmates (perhaps combined with the limited number of staff) makes adequate classification and supervision of inmates impossible.

Conclusion

While court involvement in corrections may be diminishing in many areas, even some areas protected by the Eighth Amendment, court involvement remains active in conditions of confinement cases as the number of incarcerated inmates in America continues to soar. In contrast to other areas of law, the fundamental legal tests that govern conditions of confinement have not been significantly changed since the early 1980s. The Eighth Amendment is the source of the greatest court influence in corrections and is likely to remain so for the indefinite future.

Review Questions

1. Who should make the decision concerning whether an inmate needs medical care?

2. What are the general areas a court will focus on in a conditions of confinement suit?

3. Why is crowding an important issue in conditions suits?

Notes

1. *Wilson v. Seiter*, iii S.Ct. 2321 (1991), conditions; *Hudson v. McMillian*, 112 S.Ct. 995 (1992), use of force.
2. 429 U.S. 97 (1976).
3. *Farmer v. Brennan*, 114 S.Ct. 1970 (1944).
4. American Correctional Association. 2000. *Directory of Juvenile and Adult Correctional Departments, Institutions, Agencies and Paroling Authorities*. American Correctional Association.
5. Ross, Darrell L. 1997. Section 1983 Jail Litigation, A Twenty-five Year Content Analysis. *Corrections Compendium*. 22:1
6. 101 S.Ct. 2392 (1981).
7. 111 S.Ct. 2321 (1991).
8. *Morales-Feliciano v. Parole Board of the Commonwealth of Puerto Rico*, 887 F.2d 1 (1st Cir., 1989), *Ahrens v. Thomas* 434 F.Supp. 873 (W.D. Mo., 1977).
9. *Morales-Feliciano v. Hernandez Colon*, 775 F.Supp. 487 (D. Puerto Rico, 1991).
10. 518 U.S. 343 (1996). See Ch. IV for additional discussion of the *Lewis* case, which dealt both with lower courts' relief powers and inmates' right of access to the courts.
11. *Williams v. Vincent*, 508 F.2d 541 (2d Cir., 1974).
12. *Mandel v. Doe*, 888 F.2d 783 (11th Cir., 1989).
13. *Brock v. Warren County*, 713 F.Supp. 238 (E.D. Tenn., 1989).
14. *Grass v. Sargent*, 903 F.2d 1207 (8th Cir., 1990), *Doughty v. Board of County Commissioners for County of Weld*, 731 F.Supp. 423 (D. Colo., 1989).
15. *Helling v. McKinney*, 113 S.Ct. 2475 (1993).
16. *Thomas v. Booker*, 762 F.2d 654 (8th Cir., 1985).

IX.
Suicide

In both prisons and jails, some inmates will attempt suicide. Some will succeed, despite the best efforts of administrators and staff. And lawsuits seem to follow those suicides (and many suicide attempts) almost as night follows day. The suicide problem is particularly significant in jails, where nearly 50 percent of all inmate deaths are suicides, as opposed to only about 10 percent in prisons. About three times more suicides occur in jails than in prisons.[1]

The suits will be filed claiming both civil rights violations and negligence (or other theories of recovery) under state law and will be brought either by the estate of the deceased and/or by the surviving family. Whatever legal theory may underlie these suits, their basic claims will be the same: some failure on the part of institution staff resulted in the death of the victim and that despite the victim's intention to take his or her own life, the institution in some way should have intervened to prevent the suicide.

The suits will ask for damages, and the damage awards can be high. In 1985, the city of Detroit tentatively settled a jail suicide case for $275,000. That same year, a New York City jury awarded $1,000,000 following a suicide attempt that failed. An eighteen-year-old with mental problems who was hallucinating in a jail climbed to the top of a fifteen-foot-high set of bars and dove off, fracturing his skull, partially paralyzing himself and losing his sense of smell.[2]

While the jury reacted to the facts in the New York case, an appeals court instead reacted to the law and reversed the damage award.[3] The court recognized that the defendants owed a duty of reasonable care to the plaintiff, and that what the defendants must do in a particular case depends on the risk that is reasonably perceived. (In short, the greater the risk that the institution staff perceived or reasonably should have perceived, the more the staff will be expected to have done in response to the risk.) Noting well-developed policies on restraint of inmates (which did not require restraint of a person behaving as the plaintiff), the court ruled the defendants had taken adequate precautions to protect the plaintiff. The staff had taken the victim's belt and shoelaces and placed an officer outside the holding pen.

In July 1986, a jury awarded 2.4 million dollars against the District of Columbia for what could be called a "failure to properly respond" suicide suit.[4] This case shows what a narrow margin of error jail staff may have in avoiding liability. The deceased person had been arrested for drunk driving and placed in a holding cell. He was found hanging shortly thereafter. (The victim lived for over a year without regaining consciousness.) The jury was convinced that resuscitation efforts did not begin for five minutes after the victim was found. Expert testimony showed irreversible brain damage occurs about eight minutes after oxygen is cut off from the brain. The jury believed that had efforts to revive the victim been begun sooner, he would have been saved. The point of this case is that efforts to revive a suicide victim must be begun virtually instantly, even if the victim appears dead.

Anyone working in corrections, especially jails, should bear the following basic rules in mind:

1. There will be suicides.
2. There will be lawsuits about them.

The message is clear: forewarned is forearmed. Proper anticipation and preparation for suicide attempts and for subsequent lawsuits not only will reduce the likelihood of successful suicide attempts but also will reduce the likelihood of successful suits.

Theories of Liability: Why Inmates Must Be Protected from Themselves

A suicide does not create liability. Correctional facilities and staff are not no-fault insurers of inmates who attempt suicide. But correctional staff do have a duty to protect inmates from themselves and, therefore, cannot brush off potential suicide liability simply by saying that "we can't be responsible for what someone does to himself." The key liability question is how the duty to protect is defined and what steps the institution must take to meet the duty the law creates.

Under basic tort law, the custodian has the duty to take "reasonable" steps to protect those in custody. This duty includes using due care to protect inmates from one another as well as protecting inmates from themselves. The duty owed a specific inmate in a specific situation will depend on the facts of the situation—what is reasonable for one inmate not thought to be a serious suicide threat may not be reasonable for the next inmate, whose condition is more serious.[5]

Case Study: "Deliberate Indifference" Not Easy Burden for Plaintiff

The arrestee—and later suicide victim—came into the jail with prominent scars on his wrists, inside his elbows, and on the back of his neck. These scars were shown to an officer. Failure to recognize these as signs of previous suicide attempts and to take some sort of precautions was, at worst, mere negligence. Even when the arrestee's probation officer, who knew of the suicidal tendencies and prior attempts, visited the offender in the jail but did not inform jail staff about the potential suicide problems, only negligence was shown. With only negligence being proven, the plaintiff failed to show any of the decedent's constitutional rights had been violated. *Freedman v. City of Allentown*, 853 F.2d 1111 (3rd Cir., 1988).

A duty to protect also exists under the Constitution, although courts are not of a single mind as to precisely what theory supports the duty. To some, the duty is part of the duty to provide adequate medical care. To others, it is a part of the general duty to protect.[6] While there may be interesting conceptual differences between these two theories, the differences are of greater concern to theoreticians than to practitioners. Under either a medical care or failure to protect approach, the question will be whether the defendants were deliberately indifferent to the needs of the inmates.

The deliberate indifference test requires proof of more than simple negligence (the test under most tort theories), and it would appear that if anything, the gap between negligence and deliberate indifference is growing, not shrinking. *In Partridge v. Two Unknown Police Officers*, the majority emphasized that to state a claim under a deliberate

107

indifference theory, there must be a failure to take action when there is a strong likelihood, not a mere possibility, that injury will occur.[7]

Given the lower legal burden, a plaintiff faces when suing under a tort (negligence) theory, it is likely that an increasing amount of suicide litigation will be brought under a tort theory. However, civil rights claims often will be included, if for no other reasons than to increase the possible ways of recovering and to create a possibility for the plaintiff to recover attorney's fees under 42 USC Sec. 1983.

Categories of Factual Allegations

The allegations in a suicide case usually will focus on one or more of the following areas:

1. **Failure to identify**. A failure to identify the victim as a potential suicide and to take proper steps to prevent the suicide is perhaps the most common claim. This claim may arise from such things as a failure of police to tell jail staff of an arrestee's strange behavior at the time of booking or the failure of one institution to tell another institution about an inmate's mental problems at the time the inmate is transferred. Failures on the part of staff to recognize and respond to inappropriate behavior on the part of the inmate also may be raised under this category.

   As an example of a "failure to identify" type of case, a federal appeals court found the following facts, if proven at trial, could show deliberate indifference on the part of defendants:[8] The suicide victim-to-be was arrested on suspicion of burglary and theft. On the way to the station, he tried to kick out the windows of the police car and hit his head on the divider between the front and rear seats. His father told police the arrestee had had a nervous breakdown. Police failed to tell jail staff any of this information.

   Jail staff failed to notice that the victim had been in the jail before and had attempted suicide (information available in jail clinical records). (Does this say jail staff must search their own records for this sort of information?) Two medical alert bracelets were noted, one indicating "mental." Despite all this information, no special precautions were taken. Three hours after being booked, the arrestee hanged himself in a solitary cell.[9]

Under these facts, deliberate indifference could have been shown, even though the court noted the plaintiff must show a strong likelihood of injury (not a mere possibility) and that the defendants failed to act in light of this strong possibility. It may be that one cannot show deliberate indifference in failing to identify a potential suicide candidate unless there has been either a previous threat of suicide or an actual previous attempt at suicide.[10]

2. **Failure to monitor**. A failure to monitor the victim while in the facility and thus failing to detect and respond to a suicide attempt rapidly enough often is an issue. This claim might be raised when audio or visual monitoring systems are not working at the time of the suicide, or staff do not pay attention to the audio or visual monitors, or when staff fail to make rounds at proper intervals. What is a "proper" interval may vary depending on the inmate. In extreme situations, inmates may have to be kept under constant observation by staff. Single-celling some inmates may provide the basis of a claim, despite all that has been said in favor of single celling in recent years.[11] Putting a potentially suicidal inmate in a cell with another person may help discourage the inmate from attempting suicide and increase the likelihood of a warning to facility staff should a suicide be attempted.

3. **Failure to respond**. A failure to respond properly to the suicide attempt once it is detected may be the basis of a claim. Are staff trained in what to do in the case of a suicide attempt, and do they act in accordance with their training? Is immediate emergency care provided (usually CPR)? Is additional medical care called immediately, and does it arrive in a timely fashion? (Jail staff cannot be held liable for a fire department emergency medical team being delayed in arriving, once called. But liability could be based on the jail's knowledge that emergency medical care is always some time and distance away and then failing to take steps to see that such care can be obtained more quickly.)

Allowing a hanging victim to remain hanging for a substantial period was found to be deliberate indifference to the inmate's serious medical needs, even though the officer thought the inmate was dead. In another case, a seventeen-year-old detainee hanged himself. The police chief, treating the scene as a crime scene, refused to allow officers to cut him down when they found him until the sheriff, prosecutor, and photo unit arrived. The appeals court in that case said it was an error not to allow the jury to hear an expert's opinion on whether the delay in administering CPR was a substantial factor contributing to the death of the youth.[12] The "message" from these cases is that officers need to treat any suicide as a medical emergency and respond as quickly as they can on that basis, consistent with fundamental security concerns in the institution.

Facility design can even become an issue in a suicide case. Early in 2000, the Seventh Circuit considered such a case. There were no allegations that jail staff had failed to watch the arrestee properly. The only claim was that the City of Chicago, which ran the jail, was deliberately indifferent to the safety needs of detainees because its cells were built with horizontal bars. The arrestee had hanged himself from one of these bars. Noting that the state jail standards permitted such construction and that the plaintiff did not present any evidence showing such construction was contrary to contemporary professional standards, the court ruled in favor of the city.[13]

The case mentioned earlier from New York where the inmate dove off the bars included a claim of negligence based on the high-ceilinged design, which allowed the inmate to dive from the height he did. In another case, an inmate hanged himself from overhead bars in the cell. The court ruled there was no negligence as a matter of law (thus preventing the question of the cell design from even getting to the jury) because the inmate could have hanged himself from bars on the side of the cell, as well. Had there been allegations in the case of bizarre behavior (there were none), putting an inmate in a cell with overhead bars more easily could have made cell design a relevant issue.

Finally, suicide cases may be the sort in which everything but the kitchen sink gets thrown into the complaint. In a Montana case, an arrestee hanged himself within thirty minutes of being booked on three traffic offenses. A suit by the parents alleged violations of the First, Fourth, Fifth, Sixth, Eighth, Ninth, Tenth, and Fourteenth

Amendments, as well as state claims of negligence, gross negligence, intentional inflections of emotional distress, and assault and battery.[14]

Any of the main three areas (failure to detect, failure to monitor, failure to respond) can be based either on failures of individuals to do what they should or on failures of the system to properly prepare staff for the inevitable suicide attempts. Examples of system failures might include intake screening procedures that did not require booking staff to ask questions that might show an arrestee was suicidal or failures to train staff in recognizing behavioral indicators of potential suicides. Examples of individual failures would include situations where an individual staff member failed to complete a screening questionnaire or failed to observe the inmate frequently enough.

Preparation: The Key to Liability Prevention

Given that suicide attempts are predictable in a general sense in virtually any correctional facility (especially jails), the failure to have proper policies and procedures relating to identification, monitoring, and responding can be argued to be deliberate indifference and almost certainly would show negligence on the part of administrators.

Particularly important in the jail setting is the procedure for initial screening of persons at the time of booking, since many suicides occur shortly after initial booking.[15] This screening readily can be done by booking officers and does not have to rely on mental health professionals, although obviously the results of such screening could require the prompt involvement of mental health experts. The initial screening should rely on a written screening instrument, of which many are available.[16]

Staff should be trained in recognition of symptoms of potential suicides, and procedures should exist for the referral of these persons to mental health specialists. Communication here between custody staff and mental health staff is of great importance. This communication must work in both directions. Custody staff need to be able to get information quickly to mental health personnel, but also need to be able to get information back from the mental health staff regarding the status of inmates in the cellblock, whether special precautions need to be taken, and so forth.

Monitoring procedures and facilities should be available. If mechanical monitoring (audio, video) is used, it should be kept functional. If an inmate is being monitored at some regular interval, logs should be

111

kept showing the number and times of staff contact. Mechanical monitoring (audio, video) is not a substitute for in-person monitoring.

Case Study: If Something Can Go Wrong, It Will, but Juries Can Be Fickle

A man was arrested and charged with attempted forcible rape. After a few weeks in a Louisiana jail, he told the jail nurse and jail warden that he wanted to die and that someone was trying to kill him. Later that day, he claimed he swallowed a large number of pills, although no one ever determined what he swallowed.

The jail doctor ordered the detainee taken to the hospital, where his stomach was pumped. The doctor classified him as suicidal and recommended he be taken to New Orleans for a psychiatric evaluation, which was done. The psychiatrist prepared a report, put it in an envelope, and gave it to a deputy, who brought the envelope and the inmate back to the jail. The deputy did not know what was in the envelope. He did not give it to anyone at the jail, but simply put it on the booking desk at a time when the warden was in the vicinity.

When the inmate returned to the jail, he punched an officer and tried to escape. The warden promptly put him in solitary confinement, where he committed suicide a short while later. After his death, the envelope was found and opened. The psychiatrist had diagnosed him as suicidal and recommended that suicide precautions be taken. Obviously, none were. Suit was brought by his widow and children.

Using a "deliberate indifference" test, the jury found the man's right to medical care had been violated and that the warden was responsible for the violation. But having found a constitutional violation, the jury awarded only $6,279 damages for funeral costs. *Lewis v. Parish of Terrebone*, 894 F.2d 142 (5th Cir., 1990).

Staff also should be trained in suicide response and in lifesaving skills, especially CPR. Records should show the training staff have received. Records, in the forms of logs, booking forms, incident reports, and the like also will be of great importance in documenting what staff knew of an inmate, what precautions had been taken (if any), and what the response was to the suicide attempt.

Conclusion

Suicide litigation is one of those areas of litigation where keeping a case away from a jury may be very important. A case in point is the New York case where the jury awarded $1,000,000 to the detainee who dove off the cell bars. The appeals court reversed, holding the defendants were not liable as a matter of law.

Often the suicide victim will be someone arrested for relatively minor offenses, often as a juvenile. In short, the victim may be someone for whom the jury may have a good deal of sympathy. If the victim fits this description, the jury may not be particularly impressed by the jail defendants explaining their policies and procedures and theories of jail management. Yet, if such policies and procedures are in place, records can show staff were trained in them, and that the policies and procedures were followed carefully, a court may be able to rule in defendants' favor without the case getting to the jury. But any failure in following the best policy may give the plaintiff a "but for" argument and get the case to the jury. "But for" the defendants' failure to start CPR quickly enough, the victim suffered prolonged lack of oxygen to the brain and eventually died.

The duties jail and prison administrators have toward protecting persons in their custody from themselves are relatively clear. Winning or losing a suicide suit then will depend on the facts of the case: Did the staff know what they were supposed to do, and did they do it?

Review Questions

1. Name two types of legal actions that could be brought following a suicide.

2. What are the three factual claims most likely to appear in a suicide case?

3. Give two examples of where an individual officer's failures could provide the basis for a suicide lawsuit.

Notes

1. Cohen, *Sourcebook on the Mentally Disordered Offender,* p. 67, National Institute of Corrections, 1985. For additional data about jail suicides, see Hayes and Rowan, *National Study Of Jail Suicides: Seven Years Later,* National Center on Institutions and Alternatives, February 1988.
2. *Jail and Prisoner Law Bulletin,* March 1985 and January 1986.
3. *Gordon v. City of New York,* 502 NYS 2d 215 (Supreme Court App. Div., 1986).
4. 17 *Jail and Prison Law Bulletin,* p. 11, September 1986.
5 *Civil Liability of Prison or Jail Authorities For Self-Inflicted Injury or Death of Prisoners,* 79 ALR 3rd 1210 (1977).
6. *Partridge v. Two Unknown Police Officers,* 751 F.2d 1448 (5th Cir., 1985). For sentenced inmates, the claim under either theory would be made under the Eighth Amendment (cruel and unusual punishment). For pretrial detainees, the claim would arise under the Fourteenth Amendment (due process). The functional test under either Eighth or Fourteenth Amendments basically would be the same.
7. 751 F.2d at 1453.
8. *Partridge,* see endnote 6.
9. Use of single cells for potential suicide victims, unless extraordinary staffing measures are taken, has been criticized. Multiple celling has been shown to reduce suicides, although obviously it can create other problems. Rowan, *Monograph of Suicide Prevention*, Juvenile and Criminal Justice International, Inc. Rowan is the former director of the American Medical Association's Jail Project.
10. *Edwards v. Gilbert,* 867 F.2d 1271 (11th Cir., 1989).
11. *See* endnote 7.
12. *Heflin v. Stewart County,* 958 F.2d 709 (6th Cir., 1992), *Hake v. Manchester* Township, 486 A.2d 836 (N.J., 1985).

13. *Frake v. City of Chicago,* 2000 WL 433568, (7th Cir., 2000).
14. *Strandberg v. City of Helena,* 791 F.2d 744 (9th Cir., 1986).
15. Rowan and Hayes, *Training Curriculum On Suicide Detection and Prevention In Jails and Lockups,* National Center on Institutions and Alternatives, February 1988.
16. *See* Rowan and Hayes, endnote 15. The American Correctional Association, the National Sheriff's Association, and the American Jail Association have information on screening programs and jail suicide prevention generally. Most major jails also are sources of information regarding screening programs.

X.
Use of Force

Correctional officers legally are authorized to use force against inmates in appropriate circumstances.[1] In some circumstances, even deadly force may be used. But the legal power to use force is limited, both by statute and case law. The improper use of force can expose the officer—and perhaps the agency—to liability.

Force may not be used to punish inmates. Agency rules uniformly prohibit the use of force as punishment. The officer or officers who surreptitiously beat inmates "to teach them a lesson" invite agency discipline against themselves (probably termination), as well as lawsuits by the inmate. The supervisor who turns a blind eye to this sort of improper force also may find himself or herself at the wrong end of a lawsuit for failing to properly supervise officers.

Use-of-force claims can be brought as torts or as civil rights actions. As a tort, the claim would be brought in state court and probably would be characterized as "assault and battery." The claim would be that the force was not authorized under state law or, that while some force was proper, the amount used was excessive.

Brought as a civil rights action, a use-of-force claim would assert that a constitutional right had been violated. For convicted persons, the claim would be brought under the Eighth Amendment—the force used constituted cruel and unusual punishment. For pretrial detainees (who are not protected by the Eighth Amendment), the claim would arise under the Fourteenth Amendment (due process). Under either analysis, the basic questions are the same. In either situation, the court must consider two questions, one objective, one subjective. The objective question considers the seriousness of the injury the inmate suffered. Generally speaking, if the inmate suffers no injury or only a minor injury (a *"de minimus"* injury, in legal parlance), the inmate's claim fails.

If the inmate's claim meets the objective test, then a court will consider the subjective question. Here, the question is "whether force was applied in a good-faith effort to maintain or restore discipline, or maliciously and sadistically to cause harm."[2] Courts are split on whether their focus should be on the first or second half of this test. One circuit takes the position that if force is not used in a good faith effort to maintain or restore discipline, it is virtually then by definition malicious and sadistic.[3] Other circuits focus more heavily on the nature of the force, trying to determine if it amounts to malicious and sadistic conduct.[4] More discussion of the constitutional test for evaluating use-of-force claims appears below.

Justifying Force

When is force justified? In general, force may be appropriate when, in the eyes of a reasonable correctional officer, there are no other available alternatives, and the force is used for the following reasons:

- in self-defense
- to protect others or to protect property
- to enforce prison rules and discipline
- to prevent a crime, including escapes

Deadly force requires special comment. Because of the potential consequences—loss of life—anytime deadly force is used, its proper use is more limited than nondeadly force. Because of the seriousness of the potential consequences, staff need to be very familiar with the limitation in agency policy about the use of deadly force.

Deadly force may be used in self-defense and in the protection of others from death or serious bodily harm and, in at least some cases, in the prevention of escape. Deadly force generally may not be used for the protection of property.

While it is easy to state the principles of when force may be used, it is much more difficult to provide clear guidance as to how those principles would be applied in particular cases. The basic rules listed above are not absolute. For instance, force is not always proper as a tool to enforce institutional rules, when alternatives less than force would have gotten the job done adequately. And if some force is proper, that does not mean that any amount of force is proper. While physically escorting an inmate away from a disturbance (technically, a use of force) is proper, it is not proper to strike the inmate repeatedly with a baton unless there is a sound reason for using the baton.

Most excess force litigation looks at the following basic questions:

1. Was there a need for force in the first place?
2. If some force was appropriate, was the *amount used* appropriate?
3. If force was not appropriate and/or the amount used was excessive, was the amount used so excessive as to violate the Constitution or state law?

In 1992, the Supreme Court reviewed a use-of-force case, *Hudson v. McMillian*, that arose out of a beating that occurred in a Louisiana prison. The trial court found that one officer had held an inmate being moved in the institution while another officer kicked and punched the inmate, who had been offering no resistance and was in handcuffs and shackles. A supervisor observed the incident, but did nothing to intervene, and, in fact, the court found the supervisor had expressly condoned the force being used. The court also found there was absolutely no need for force being used and that the officers were motivated by malice. The inmate sustained some injuries, but they were not serious. He was awarded $800 in damages.

The court of appeals reversed the district court decision. It felt that unless the inmate could show he had sustained a "significant injury," he could not prove that he had been subjected to cruel and unusual punishment, regardless of how unnecessary the force was.

The Supreme Court reversed, saying that it was error to insist that a beating victim prove "significant injury" in order to state a claim for relief.[5] The Court said that in excess force cases, the proper question was whether the inmate had suffered the "wanton and unnecessary infliction of pain."

The Court further defined the phrase "wanton and unnecessary infliction of pain," saying that in situations involving the use of force, which often may be emergencies (although the facts of the *Hudson* case did not involve an emergency), the question is "whether force was applied in a good faith effort to maintain or restore discipline or maliciously and sadistically for the very purpose of causing harm."[6] This test maximizes the discretion available to institution officials and minimizes the extent to which courts can review use of force situations. The Court further explained its "malicious and sadistic" test by indicating it has five factors which a court should evaluate in reviewing a force incident:

1. Was there a need to use any force?
2. What was the amount of force used?
3. What injuries were inflicted, if any? (While significant injury is not required, the extent of any injuries are relevant and should be considered. The inmate who suffers little if any injury will have a difficult time winning an excess force case. Questions about the nature and extent of injuries are important in deciding if the inmate's claim meets the objective component in the use-of-force analysis).
4. What was the threat perceived by responsible correctional officials?
5. What efforts to temper the use of force were made?

The *Hudson* decision took its "malicious and sadistic" test from an earlier Supreme Court decision, which created and applied the test in the setting of a prison riot.[7] Application of this test outside the riot-emergency context, especially in a case which involved officers beating an inmate, was surprising because the effect of the *Hudson* decision is to reduce judicial oversight over use-of- force incidents. A use-of-force incident could be criticized under all five of the factors identified in the *Hudson* case yet still not sink to the level of being "malicious and sadistic." However, excessive uses of force still may violate the rights of inmates.

Kneeing an inmate twice in the groin as a first response to the inmate's aggressiveness during booking, instead of using other more humane means of physical restraint, violated the rights of the inmate and led to a damage award of over $56,000, including $25,000 in punitive damages.[8] In another case, a court of appeals said that an officer's use of a stun gun against an inmate locked in his cell as a response to the inmate's refusal to clean his cell violated the rights of the inmate.[9]

As a practical matter, a court analyzing an excess force claim under the test from the *Hudson* case usually makes up its mind after considering the first three of the five important factors listed in *Hudson*. Thus, if there is only a *de minimus* injury, the claim fails on the "injury" question. Or if there is a clear relationship between the need for some force and the amount actually used, the claim will typically fail. On the "need" and "amount" questions, which are closely related, an officer who follows a well-established force continuum is in a very good position to defend his or her use of force.

Case Study: Unchecked Use of Force Creates Liability for Agency, Not Just Officers

No one is happy until they get their morning coffee. Or so it seems. An inmate mouthed off to an officer about not getting his coffee. When the officer did not respond, the inmate reached through the bars and pushed the officer in the back. The officer then responded by getting a fire hose and hosing the inmate, who remained the entire time locked in his single cell. Other officers squirted tear gas on the inmate and beat him with nightsticks. Sixty-nine stitches were required to repair the damage.

This force violated the rights of the inmate. Evidence also showed that the warden condoned the use of fire hoses against inmates in single cells who did not present any direct threat to staff. The warden once had approved hosing a handcuffed inmate locked in a cell. Recommendations from a special commission to discontinue using fire hoses were rejected. While it was not completely clear if the head of the agency knew of the use of fire hoses, it was clear he should have. Under these circumstances, both the warden and the agency director were found liable, along with the officers actually involved in the incident. The inmate was awarded more than $32,000 in damages. *Slakan v. Porter*, 737 F.2d 368 (4th Cir., 1984).[10]

Many correctional agencies have adopted a "force continuum" to provide guidance to staff in force situations. The continuum indicates what the officer's range of appropriate response alternatives are when an inmate's behavior falls into one of several broad categories. Thus, if the inmate is passively resistive, the officer's range of alternatives is more limited than if the inmate is engaged in life-threatening behavior. By acting consistently with the agency's force continuum, the officer usually will be able to say "my actions were taken in accordance with

121

Case Study: Hog-tieing and the Mentally Disturbed Inmate

A short, heavy, middle-aged man was arrested for bizarre, threatening behavior. Police recognized him as probably mentally disturbed, and he was a regular at the jail. He passively refused to cooperate in the booking process. One officer began to physically move the man back to the booking station when another ordered to "take him down." Several officers then took the man to the ground and put him in a "kick stop restraint," a device which tied his hands and feet together behind his back. The court's opinion does not indicate officers made any attempt to deal with the inmate short of immediately placing him in restraints. Nor does the response appear to have taken into consideration the man's history of mental problems, although his behavior was clearly abnormal and jail staff knew his history.

Although the kick stop restraint was commonly used in the jail, none of the officers or supervisors had been trained in use of the device or were aware that the manufacturer cautioned against placing a person in the device face down because of a risk of suffocation. A video showed a supervisor placing his weight on the arrestee's back while other officers bound the man's hands and feet together. Medical experts testified this caused the man's death by asphyxiation. Other manufacturer's cautions were ignored.

Within minutes after the man was hog tied and placed in a cell, he was dead.

The man's estate filed suit against the city that operated the jail and a large number of individual officers. After a twenty-seven-day trial, the jury returned a damages verdict of nearly $10,000,000 against all of the defendants jointly. In addition, the jury entered punitive damages awards against eight individual defendants, in amounts ranging from $225,000 to $1,000,000. In total, the damages awards came to nearly 13 million dollars! *Swans v. City of Lansing*, 65 F.Supp. 2d 625 (W.D. Mich., 1998).

agency policy which in turn reflects a carefully thought out way of balancing the amount of force used against the need for the use of force."

Weapons, Special Holds, and "Inherently Dangerous Instrumentalities"

Batons, gas, tasers, stun belts, hoses, choke or sleeper holds, or other special forms of manual or physical restraint may not be classified as deadly force, but still may carry the potential for serious injury. If used properly, they can reduce the risk of injury to both the officer and the inmate. They are, however, capable of being abused and becoming a means of improperly punishing the inmate.

In the case study in this chapter, one of the reasons the court imposed liability against the agency director was due to the lack of any policy describing the use of what the court called "inherently dangerous instrumentalities," such as the fire hoses. Firearms and other instruments that have the potential of inflicting very serious harm also would be included in the category of "inherently dangerous instrumentalities." The law may give staff using such techniques or instruments an especially high duty to use them properly. So, a lawsuit might focus on two somewhat different questions: (1) Was there a sufficient justification to use, for instance, a firearm? and (2) Was the firearm used in a careful way? The person who might bring the latter claim is the innocent bystander who was shot by mistake.

Sometimes an injury or death may result from a practice that no one realized was dangerous. What if an inmate dies after being hit with a taser? Neck holds, now usually seen as a form of deadly force, did not used to be classified as such. Only after several inmates died as a result of neck holds did many agencies classify neck holds as deadly force. If there were no notice, the practice was likely to cause such death or injury, liability is not likely. But after death or injury occurs once, is an agency on notice about the practice? What if death occurs a second time? The more times the "unexpected" occurs (such as death resulting from the use of neck holds), the more an agency will be expected to be aware that special precautions and training may be necessary.

Restraints

Inmates may be restrained physically for good cause. However, restraints should be used in accordance with a carefully drawn policy and their use closely monitored to assure they are not being used improperly. Where it appears restraints are being used for excessively long periods or applied in ways that may injure an inmate or inflict unnecessary pain, courts have intervened. For example:

Following a suicide attempt, an inmate was "hog-tied" in three-point restraints in a squatting position and left that way for a week. The court said that the prolonged use of the three-way restraints following the inmate's suicide attempt, plus the lack of medical review or treatment and denial of even basic amenities such as personal hygiene and toilet usage violated the inmate's rights. Compensatory damages were imposed against various individual officers, and punitive damages were imposed on the official responsible for operation of the jail and against the county.[11]

Areas of concern regarding use of restraints include (1) the decision to place an inmate in restraints: who makes it, and in accordance with what criteria? (2) the types of restraints used, (3) how long an inmate remains in restraints, (4) monitoring both to determine if the need remains for restraints and of the inmate's general safety, comfort, hygiene, and medical/mental health condition.

Deadly Force and Escapes

Courts have not given clear guidance on the question of the use of deadly force to prevent escapes. Perhaps the largest issue which is not yet clearly resolved is whether deadly force can be used to prevent any escape (perhaps assuming no other alternative is immediately available) or whether some assessment must be made about the dangerousness of the inmate attempting to escape. Obviously, asking the officer in most escape situations to make such an assessment is to impose a very difficult task on the officer, who may know nothing about the inmate, except that he is trying to escape. One reason for this uncertainty is that there have been very few cases involving the use of deadly force against escapees. Another reason is that different legal tests are used to review any use-of-force claim depending on whom the force is used: a suspect (Fourth Amendment), an arrestee (Fourth Amendment), a pretrial detainee (Fourteenth Amendment), or a convicted inmate (Eighth Amendment).[12]

Questions of state law may further complicate the legal analysis of use of deadly force. For example, under the laws of one state, it is justifiable homicide for a peace officer to use deadly force (and kill an inmate) to prevent the escape of an inmate from a prison or jail. However, the statute says that deadly force generally may not be used against an escaping jail inmate unless the inmate was "arrested for, charged with, or convicted of a felony."[13] This sort of issue should be addressed in the agency's deadly force policies.

Use of deadly force not only raises potential liability issues regarding the person the force is used against, but it also can involve liability issues regarding other persons who may be injured by a shot that misses its intended target or a bullet that ricochets. The legal uncertainty in this area can be confusing for staff who may be expected to use deadly force. In light of this confusion, the best advice for the officer with deadly force responsibilities is to be very familiar with guidelines of facility policies regarding the use of deadly force.

Documentation

The quality of records an agency keeps may be critical in defending a use-of-force case. The details of any use-of-force incident are important to the supervisor of the officer(s) involved in the incident so the supervisor can be sure the force was used appropriately. (Ignoring abusive use of force can expose the supervisor to liability.) Should there be a lawsuit filed, the records can help the officer remember what happened during the incident and even may be entered as evidence at trial. Therefore, detailed use-of-force reports can be very important to protect the officer.

Three different types of records can be important.

1. **Incident reports**. First and foremost, officers involved in a use-of-force incident should prepare detailed reports of their actions. These reports should address not only why force was used, but also should describe the actual amount used.

   But to be useful, the reports must be detailed. Simply writing that "only necessary force was used" is of no benefit since such a phrase only states the officer's opinion. What is important is that the officer preparing the report include enough detail so that the reader of the report (be it a supervisor or a judge or a jury) can draw an opinion from the report itself as to whether force was properly used at all and whether the amount used was appropriate under the circumstances. Reports that do not allow this sort of third-party evaluation should be returned to the officer for rewriting.

2. **Videotapes**. Since the late 1970s, many agencies videotape all use-of-force incidents where time and circumstances allow. A videotape shows precisely the amount of force used and can be very impressive to a judge or jury.

   While the videotape in the kick stop restraint case discussed earlier in this chapter was used successfully against officers, this is the exception. It is far more common that a video will show that officers acted properly. Many administrators also say that the presence of the video camera helps deter some officers from using excessive force. Even where there are not lawsuits about force usage, videotapes give the administrator an excellent tool for evaluating uses of force against the expectations of agency policy.

3. **Medical records**. It is common to have inmates promptly examined by medical personnel immediately after force is used on the inmate. This examination serves two purposes. It gives the inmate prompt treatment for any injuries, reducing the likelihood of a suit regarding delayed or denied medical care. It also gives the institution an accurate record of any injuries (or the lack of any injuries). This evidence can be useful in rebutting later inmate claims about serious injury.

Can Force Be Avoided?

The best way to avoid a use-of-force lawsuit is to avoid using force. While obviously force is the only alternative in some situations, in many instances the officer or officers with interpersonal skills can de-escalate a situation and avoid any use of force, even though legally the use of force might have been justified. Likewise, an officer whose interpersonal skills are weak actually may worsen a situation and create the need for force when it could have been avoided. Any time force is used, both the inmate and the officers involved are at risk. The greater the officer's skill in resolving situations without the use of any force, the more the safety of all concerned is increased.

Conclusion

As with many other areas of institutional operation that involve inmate rights, protection against successful claims regarding improper use of restraints will depend on having a sound policy or other written directives, which provides guidance for staff, training for staff around the requirements of the policy, documentation regarding uses of force, and strong supervision to assure the policy is followed properly.

Some legal uncertainties remain regarding the use of force (such as the questions around using deadly force to prevent escapes). However, the fundamental principles governing almost all use-of-force situations for line staff are clear.

1. Policies should govern use of force and should be carefully followed.
2. Force may not be used for punishment.
3. Force only should be used when there are no other reasonable alternatives under the situation.
4. Documentation describing use-of-force incidents is important and should be carefully reviewed by supervisors.
5. A court reviewing use-of-force situations generally will examine those from the perspective of a reasonable correctional officer, acting in light of the facts as they appeared to the officer who actually used the force.

Review Questions

1. May deadly force be used to protect property?

2. In a constitutional excess force case, what five questions will a court ask?

3. Give two reasons why detailed use-of-force reports are important.

Notes

1. For a more detailed discussion *see* Hemmens, C. and Eugene Atherton. 1999. *Use of Force: Current Practice and Policy.* Lanham, Maryland: American Correctional Association.
2. *Hudson v. McMillian*, 112 S.Ct. 995 (1992).
3. *Blyden v. Mancusi*, 186 F.3d 252, 262 (2d Cir.,1999).
4. *Fuentes v. Wagner*, 206 F.3d 335 (3rd Cir., 2000).
5. *Hudson v. McMillan*, 112 S.Ct. 995 (1992).
6. 112 S.Ct. at 998.
7 *Whitley v. Albers*, 106 S.Ct. 1078 (1986).
8. Culver by and through *Bell v. Fowler*, 862 F.Supp. 369 (M.D. Ga., 1994).
9. *Hickey v. Reeder*, 12 F.3d 754 (8th Cir., 1993).
10 .Note that this case was decided in 1984. Since that time, the Supreme Court has decided that officials cannot be held liable on the basis of what they "should have known." *See* discussion of *Farmer v. Brennan*, 511 U.S. 825 (1994), in Ch. 8.
11. *Jones v. Thompson*, 818 F.Supp. 1263 (S.D. Ind., 1993).
12. See Boston, John and Daniel Manville. 1995. *Prisoner's Self-Help Litigation Manual*. Oceana Publications, p. 103.
13. Revised Code of Washington, Section 9A.16.040(c)(iii).

XI.
The Fourteenth Amendment: Due Process and Equal Protection

The Fourteenth Amendment to the U.S. Constitution reads, in part:

". . . nor shall any state deprive any person of life, liberty, or property, without due process of law; nor deny to any person within its jurisdiction the equal protection of the laws."

In other words, when the state (which includes cities and counties) proposes to take away someone's life, liberty, or property, the state must provide "due process of law" to the subject of the proposed deprivation. Usually, this means the state must go through certain procedures as part of the deprivation decision (the "process" that is "due").

The concept of equal protection means generally that groups of persons that are similar must be treated similarly by the government, unless the government can justify treating the similar groups differently. Thus, equal protection does not outlaw discrimination between groups, but does demand that discrimination be justified. Depending on what the reason for discriminating between two like groups is, it may be very difficult for the state to justify the discrimination. For instance, racial discrimination is very difficult to justify. But treating offenders differently based on their prior criminal records would not be as difficult to justify.

The concepts of due process and equal protection entered the U.S. Constitution as far as the states were concerned after the Civil War and are intended to assure that the government treats persons fairly. The amendment largely deals with how decisions are made that affect the life, liberty, or property of persons in this country. But it also sometimes simply prohibits some government actions and demands that similar groups of persons be treated the same, unless the government can justify treating them differently.

The Fourteenth Amendment applies only to the states—it does not regulate the power of the federal government. However, the Fifth Amendment to the Constitution also has a due process clause that does apply to the federal government.

Procedural Due Process in General

Most due process issues involve what is called procedural due process. This concept focuses on what procedures must accompany the decision to take away life, liberty, or property. When a court is concerned about procedural due process, it is far more concerned with the procedural steps the state goes through in making a decision than with what the final decision is. (It is not what you do, it is how you do it.) The goal of procedural due process is fairness: by requiring the state to go through certain procedures (which usually involve notice to the person of the proposed deprivation and some form of a hearing), the person is protected from arbitrary actions of government, actions that perhaps have no factual justification or that simply may be illegal. By going through certain procedures, the following can be determined better:

- if the facts really are as the government claims them to be (For example, did the inmate really violate a disciplinary rule, or did a parolee really violate a condition of parole?)
- if the government has the legal authority to make the deprivation it proposes (For example, do institution rules allow a loss of good time to be imposed as a penalty for violating a particular rule?)

The amount of process required varies from one type of situation to another. Just as with other constitutional rights, courts try to balance the individual's interest in having more procedural rights and the severity of the potential loss the person is facing against the government's interest in being able to make decisions quickly and efficiently. Under this balancing approach, the procedural protections that protect the person facing civil commitment as being mentally ill and dangeous to others (a severe loss of liberty) are much greater than those afforded a parolee in a parole revocation hearing (parole is seen as only a form of conditional liberty). The protections afforded an inmate in a prison or jail disciplinary hearing are even less than in a parole revocation hearing.

In general, the greater the potential loss the individual faces, the greater the need for more procedural protections to assure that sufficient factual and legal reasons exist to justify the loss. Outside an institutional setting, a free person normally would expect the following sorts of procedural protections to be available if the government attempted to take away the person's liberty or property:

- a hearing, at which the government would have to prove its case for deprivation
- advance notice of the hearing, including some detail of the charges, so the person could have time to prepare a defense to the charges
- a neutral judge or other decision maker
- the right to call witnesses on his or her own behalf
- the right to cross-examine witnesses testifying against the person
- the right to the assistance of a lawyer
- a decision that indicates what facts the decision maker is relying on and that gives reasons to justify it (This decision would either be in writing or maintained in some form of oral record that could be reproduced.)
- an appeal of the decision to higher authority, usually the courts

When Is "Process" Due?

Every procedural due process issue begins with the same question: Does the Fourteenth Amendment apply to a particular type of decision that affects an inmate? Does the decision involve potentially taking a liberty or property interest away from the inmate? Inmates have very few "property interests" in prison, so the most common question is whether a decision deprives an inmate of a "liberty interest." As is discussed in detail in the next section, inmate discipline is the most common area where due process protections must be followed. But what about other types of decisions which, in at least some respects, could be seen as taking away something of value to the inmate? These might include placing the inmate in administrative segregation (where

conditions and privileges are typically very similar to disciplinary segregation), or removing an inmate from a program, or transferring the
inmate from one institution to another.

The question of "when is process due" also has been a frustrating
one for officials, since the Supreme Court has not been consistent in the
way it answers the question. Some actions of correctional officials,
such as involuntarily medicating a mentally ill inmate, are inherently
protected by the due process clause of the Fourteenth Amendment.[1]
Most decisions, which affect an inmate, do not rise to this level of significance, but they still may be protected by due process, if the state has
created a liberty interest.

In 1983, the Supreme Court said that to determine if the state had
created a liberty interest around a particular type of decision (such as
the decision to place an inmate in administrative segregation), courts
must examine the language of the institution rules governing that decision.[2] This concept was difficult to understand and apply, but, in general terms, it said that if the agency had limited its discretion to make
the decision by saying it could only act when it found that certain facts
or conditions existed, a liberty interest had been created, and the decision had to be accompanied by limited due process protections. Under
this test, the seriousness of the loss was not a relevant consideration in
deciding if due process applied or not—only the language of the rule or
policy governing the decision was important.

In *Hewitt*, the Court said that the due process clause did not inherently apply to the decision to place an inmate in administrative segregation. Applying its language-focused test for "state created liberty
interests," the Court held that Pennsylvania rules did create a liberty
interest. The decision to place an inmate in administrative segregation
had to be accompanied by minimal procedural protections, including
giving notice to the inmate of the proposed decision and giving the
inmate an opportunity to respond, either orally or in writing.

Because the test from *Hewitt* looked only at the language of a rule,
and not at the seriousness of the loss the inmate suffered, litigation over
very trivial types of decisions was not uncommon. For instance, in one
case, the inmate claimed a due process interest in receiving a tray lunch
rather than a sack lunch. He won at the district court level, but lost
when the case got to the court of appeals.[3]

Thirteen years after it had adopted the language-focused test, the
Supreme Court abandoned it. In *Sandin v. Conner*,[4] the court decided

that the language-oriented test had become a disincentive to officials wanting to write rules or policies governing various types of decisions. Consider the decision to place an inmate in administrative segregation. Under the language-oriented test, if officials adopted no restricting or controlling rules concerning what would permit an inmate to be placed in administrative segregation, no due process protections would apply. But if the officials adopted rules (such as saying "an inmate may be placed in administrative segregation only under the following circumstances . . ."), due process protections could arise. Adopting a rule could mean officials increased their liability exposure. The Court also felt the old rule brought federal courts too much into the day-to-day decision making in prisons and jails. The Court cited the sack lunch case mentioned previously as an example of this type of problem.

The Court replaced the old test with one which is entirely different. Now, a liberty interest will be created only if the decision results in an "atypical and significant deprivation in relation to the normal incidents of prison life." As with many new legal tests which come from the Supreme Court, it is not clear what an "atypical and significant deprivation" is. We know from the *Sandin* decision that thirty days in disciplinary segregation is not such a deprivation. Lower court decisions, which have interpreted the phrase, tell us that much longer periods in disciplinary segregation also are not so substantial as to trigger due process protections.

Under the "atypical" test, the decision to place an inmate in administrative segregation probably will not be protected by due process. Despite uncertainties about the meaning of the new rule, in general, it should result in fewer court decisions mandating decisions be accompanied with due process protections.

Due Process and the Disciplinary Process

Over the years, the main area where procedural due process has been important in prisons or jails is in the disciplinary process. Discipline is vital to preserving security and safety in a correctional facility. If inmates are not held accountable for following certain basic rules of behavior, chaos could result. So, the institution has a strong interest in being able to enforce disciplinary rules quickly and effectively.

On the other side of the balance, inmates have an interest in not being punished for rule violations they did not commit. Violation of an institution rule can carry serious consequences for an inmate, including losing the level of freedom and privileges associated with being in an institution's general population or in a particular custody level in exchange for segregation. A rule violation may affect directly an inmate's release date if it results in a loss or denial of good time. So, inmates may have certain "liberty interests" at stake in the disciplinary process.

Due Process Applied

In 1974, the Supreme Court was asked to balance the competing interests of the institution and of inmates and to decide if due process protections applied to prison (or jail) disciplinary processes and, if due process did apply, specifically what sort of procedures were necessary.

In *Wolff v. McDonnell,*[5] the Court ruled that where state law created a right to good time and that where good time could be forfeited only for serious misbehavior, some due process protections were necessary "to ensure that the state-created right is not arbitrarily abrogated."

In *Wolff*, the Court also decided what sort of procedural protections the state had to provide in the disciplinary process. Where loss of good time (a serious sanction) was potentially involved, the hearing process had to include the following elements:

- a *hearing* at which the inmate has the right to be present. The inmate can, by words or his or her behavior, waive the right to be present at the hearing.
- *advance written notice* of the charges, given to the inmate at least twenty-four hours in advance of the hearing. More than twenty-four hours could be required if the facts and circumstances of a particular case were such that twenty-four hours was not enough time for the inmate to prepare for the hearing. The notice should include details about the time and place of the alleged incident and some other details about what the officer preparing the infraction believes occurred. This detail is necessary to allow the inmate a reasonable opportunity to know what he or she is charged with doing so that a defense can be prepared.

- the opportunity for the inmate to *call witnesses and present evidence* on his or her own behalf, except when it can be shown that to allow this, in the Supreme Court's words, would "be unduly hazardous to constitutional safety or correctional goals." Where the inmate requests that a particular witness be called and that request is denied, it will be the institution's burden to justify the denial later, if the inmate sues about the denial. Therefore, it becomes important that some sort of record be made of the reasons for a denial. Facility disciplinary rules normally will provide more detail regarding what may justify denying a witness.

- *assistance*—sometimes. Inmates do not, under any circumstances, have a right to a lawyer in a disciplinary hearing, even if criminal charges may be pending against the inmate.[6] But under some circumstances, they have a right to assistance. Where the inmate is illiterate or where the complexity of the issues makes it unlikely that the inmate will be able to collect and present the evidence necessary for an adequate comprehension of the case, the inmate is entitled to be assisted by someone. This assistant may be another inmate, a staff member, or other person. The institution largely can control who serves as assistants and can choose, for instance, not to allow inmates to serve in this role.

The precise role of the assistant will vary depending on the reasons that led to the appointment of the assistant in the first place. Thus, if an assistant is appointed to assist an inmate simply because the inmate cannot read, the role may be limited to reading various documents to the inmate. But if the assistant is appointed because the inmate is intellectually not able to understand the hearing process and the issues involved, then the assistant may have to take much more responsibility for investigating and presenting the entire case for the inmate.

There may be a duty to appoint an assistant in some cases even where the inmate does not ask for help, since some of the reasons why an assistant is needed also might be the reasons why the inmate did not ask for assistance. The hearing officer should be alert to the possible need for assistants in cases and should appoint them where he or she feels there may be a question about the inmate's ability to present his or her own case.

- *impartial tribunal.* The hearing officer or board must be impartial. If someone is a victim in or a witness to the incident that led to the infraction being charged (or involved with its investigation), the person may not serve as a hearing officer in that hearing. Similarly, if a hearing officer has some personal bias for or against an inmate, he or she should step down. That an inmate has filed a lawsuit against a hearing officer does not require automatic disqualification, but under some circumstances, a lawsuit could raise questions about a hearing officer's impartiality. This would depend on such things as the specific issues in the suit (Were they a direct attack on the officer's discretion? Were they quite personal?) and perhaps the result of the suit, if it had come to an end (Was the officer found liable?).

The fact that a hearing officer may have heard about an incident prior to the hearing (something that is almost inevitable with serious incidents, particularly in smaller facilities) does not disqualify the person. However, the decision obviously must be based only on the information presented at the hearing, not institution scuttlebutt picked up over coffee.

- *written decision.* There must be a written statement by the fault finder (the hearing officer or committee) "as to the evidence relied on and reasons" for the decision. By writing down what evidence the hearing officer believed to be true and indicating why one sanction was selected out of the typical range of sanctions, other agencies or officials (such as paroling authorities or classification committees) can understand the violation better and are less likely to make incorrect decisions about the offender based on a misunderstanding of the infraction. A written statement also allows others to review the decision for its correctness. These "others" might include supervisors within the institution or agency, as well as the court.

A written decision that simply indicates the inmate was guilty or "guilty based on all the evidence" often will not be acceptable. If the evidence was conflicting, as is the case when the officer says the inmate committed the infraction and the inmate and perhaps the inmate's witnesses say the inmate did not, guilty cannot be based on "all the evidence."[7] Obviously, the hearing officer believed some of the evidence and did not believe some. The written decision simply should review what the officer believed to be true.

When Do *Wolff* Requirements Apply?

Language in the *Wolff* opinion indicated that the Court intended its holding to apply not only when a disciplinary hearing could result in good time being taken away from an inmate, but also when the inmate faced a term in segregation. Virtually all prisons and jails in the country interpreted the case in this way.

In a 1995 decision, *Sandin v. Conner*, the Court indicated that it no longer felt that the requirements of *Wolff* or, indeed, any lesser due process requirements, applied to a disciplinary hearing which resulted in a thirty-day segregation sanction.[8] The *Sandin* decision does not indicate whether a longer disciplinary segregation penalty might require some due process requirements. Courts consistently have applied the *Sandin* result to exempt segregation sanctions considerably longer than thirty days from due process review, but some courts have suggested that a long enough sanction—perhaps over a year—still would require a full "*Wolff* hearing."[9]

Early cases following *Sandin* left a question of whether full *Wolff* protections still applied to pretrial detainees facing disciplinary proceedings involving a short segregation sanction. At least one federal appeals court held that *Wolff* still applied in this context.[10] As these words are written five years after that decision, this issue remains unresolved.

A question which arose under *Wolff* was what form of due process, if any, was required for minor infractions. Sandin answers this question by saying that unless a disciplinary sanction imposes an "atypical and significant deprivation (on the inmate) in relation to the normal incidents of prison life," no due process protections are required. *Sandin* therefore leaves agencies to address the question of what disciplinary procedures they wish to follow not only for very minor infractions, but also for more serious ones, which may carry a maximum penalty of some time in segregation, but which do not directly affect an inmate's release date.

No right to confront or cross-examine

The Court in *Wolff* refused to allow the inmate the right to confront or cross-examine witnesses against him or her. In general, the Court felt that cross-examination would tend to make the hearings longer and more difficult to manage. In particular, the Court was concerned that requiring cross-examination of inmate informants either would put those persons in serious danger or simply cut off inmates as a source of information.

In refusing to impose a right to counsel or a right to cross-examine witnesses, the Supreme Court left two of the most traditional components of due process off the list of procedural rights that must be given to inmates in disciplinary hearings. The Court did this because of the unique problems associated with running a jail or prison disciplinary system. The Court felt the balance tipped strongly in favor of the institution in the right to counsel and the right to cross-examine witnesses, despite their historic part in what has been perceived of as a "fair" hearing.

Inmate silence

The Fifth Amendment right against self-incrimination does not apply in disciplinary hearings. Thus, if an inmate refuses to testify, the inmate's silence can be used as an indicator of guilt. However, silence alone cannot prove guilt.[11]

Confidential informants

By refusing to require that inmates in disciplinary hearings be allowed to confront and cross-examine persons testifying against them, the Supreme Court opened the door for the use of information in hearings from anonymous informants. It is literally possible for an inmate to be charged and found guilty in a disciplinary hearing without knowing virtually any of the details of the charge, the source of the charge, and without hearing any direct testimony about the violation.

The ability to consider information from anonymous informants and to withhold both the name of the informant and the detail of the information (when revealing that detail would identify its source) carries with it the serious possibility of abuse. One inmate with a grudge against another may make up a story about a rule violation. Rumor about an inmate's guilt may become fact in a hearing when a charged inmate has no way to rebut the "evidence" since he or she may not even know what the evidence is.

But informant information may be almost the only way information from inmates can be used in hearings, since inmates seldom tolerate "snitches," and the inmate who testifies openly against another places himself or herself in serious danger. If little or no inmate information could be used in hearings, the disciplinary process could be seriously damaged, since many rule violations are not witnessed by staff, but may be witnessed only by inmates.

In an attempt to strike a balance between the potential for abuse from informant testimony and the institution's need to be able to consider information from inmates in the disciplinary process, courts have imposed limitations on how and when informant information may be used. The weight of these limitations falls primarily on hearing officers, but also indirectly on other staff who may bring informant information to the hearing. Unless the information is presented properly, it may not be considered. If it is considered improperly, a court is likely to overturn the results of the hearing and also may impose damages against the hearing officer or others involved in the hearing process and may impose additional requirements, making it even more difficult to consider informant information.

There are two basic requirements that must be met for informant information to be properly considered.[12]

1. **Reliability**. The hearing officer must be convinced the informant is reliable. An officer coming to the hearing and stating "I have information from a reliable informant that . . ." is not enough, because this shows only the officer's conclusion about reliability. The officer must be prepared to explain to the hearing officer (out of the presence of the charged inmate) why the source is a reliable one. Then, when the hearing officer has facts, not just conclusions, to consider, he or she can decide if the informant is reliable.

   Where the hearing officer is convinced the informant is generally reliable, the specific information can be considered, and the second requirement arises.

2. **Credibility**. Assuming the informant is generally reliable, the next question is whether the specific information offered is believable enough to prove, or help prove, guilt. If the informant

information is corroborated by other evidence in the hearing, it gains credibility. The more detailed the information is, the more credible it becomes. Unless the informant was an eye-witness to the incident, the information is suspect. Normally hearsay information ("Well, I didn't see the assault, but another inmate who did told me it happened this way.") should not be considered. An exception to this rule might be where the hearsay is actually an admission by the charged inmate ("Well, I didn't see the incident, but the charged inmate told me he did it.") Again, the hearing officer is the one who must be convinced that the information is credible.

Sometimes, the reliability and credibility determinations will blend together, but generally, the hearing officer must decide if the information is or is not believable both in light of the nature of the information itself and its source.

Case Study: White Segregation

White inmates at the Pontiac Correctional Center in Illinois sued, claiming the large percentage of white inmates in protective custody violated their equal protection rights to be free from racial segregation. Although whites made up only 12 percent of the total institution population, 40 percent of the white population was in protective custody. The plaintiffs claimed this was the result of the administration being too tolerant of gangs (which were virtually either all black or Hispanic).

The court rejected the claim, saying that unless the plaintiffs could show intentional discrimination by the administration, their equal protection claim must fail. Despite its legal conclusion, the court was very critical of the gang policies of the administration, which the court believed had led to a very serious problem, even though it did not violate the equal protection clause. *David K. v. Lane*, 839 F.2d 1265 (7th Cir., 1988).

Evidence and the Reporting Officer

Due process does allow federal courts to review the sufficiency of the evidence in a disciplinary hearing, but that review is not very demanding. Where the record of a hearing shows there was "some evidence" on which the hearing officer could have relied in making a finding of guilt, due process is satisfied. The reviewing judge is not allowed to second-guess the hearing officer. Even if the judge would not have found guilt on the basis of the evidence, if there is "some evidence," the decision must stand.[13] State law may permit state courts to review the sufficiency of the evidence more closely.

A continuing issue with disciplinary hearings is whether the reporting officer should, or must, be present to testify. Courts have not given a clear, absolute ruling on this issue. In general, the more complicated the issues in the hearing, the more important it is for the officer to testify in person. Where the factual questions in the hearing are quite simple (as is often the case), and where the officer has written a clear, complete report to support the charge, the officer's presence is less important.

Basing a finding of guilt just on a poorly written report, where the inmate presents a plausible defense that the report may not directly respond to (such as mistaken identity or facts not addressed in the report), invites court intervention in the disciplinary process.

Making a Record

It is unlikely a hearing decision will be overturned because it fails to meet the "some evidence" test. What is more likely is that a decision may be overturned because the record (which is usually all the reviewing court has to consider) is not clear or detailed enough to allow the court to tell what evidence the hearing officer relied on or what was the basis for key decisions, such as denial of a witnesses' request.

"The record" consists of all the paperwork generated by a hearing and any tape recording (or written transcript) of the hearing itself. If something is not "in the record," a court may assume it did not happen. For example, in one case an inmate was charged with possession of marijuana. The evidence consisted of a bag of what was identified as marijuana, which was found in the pocket of a shirt hanging in the inmate's cell. The hearing and the subsequent lawsuit focused largely on how the material in the bag could be identified as marijuana. (Could an officer identify it based on his experience and training, or must a chemical test of some sort be done?) While the court said the officer's identification was sufficient, the court threw out the hearing because the record failed to show that anyone in the hearing identified the bag of marijuana everyone in the hearing was looking at as the bag found in the inmate's shirt.[14] A trivial oversight? Probably so. But nevertheless, it was fatal to the hearing.

Where tape recordings of the hearings are not available (either because tapes were not made or were destroyed before the suit challenging the hearing result was filed), the court is limited to considering the written record, especially the written decision made by the hearing officer. The record will be the basis not only of a court review of the sufficiency of the evidence, but also of virtually every other discretionary decision the hearing officer makes that is of legal significance: Was there a sufficient reason to deny a witness?[15] Was the informant reliable and credible? Should an assistant have been appointed? A hearing that, in fact, met all the procedural requirements, correctly decided the inmate was guilty, and imposed an appropriate sanction can be thrown out unless the record is sufficient to establish those facts.

Remember that there probably are more decisions made that have potential constitutional importance in disciplinary hearings than in any other part of prison or jail operation. But these decisions almost all deal with procedural questions—"technicalities" to many who work in the institution. To institution staff, the important part of a disciplinary hearing is the result: Is the inmate guilty and, if so, what penalty should be imposed? But a court will be concerned about the procedural issues and the quality of the record—the "technicalities." So, unless the institution can demonstrate, almost always through the hearing record, that the procedural requirements were met, the hearing result may be a lost case.

Involuntary Medication

An inmate is diagnosed as mentally ill. The mental health experts feel the inmate may be dangerous to himself or others. Line staff who must deal with the inmate reach similar conclusions, based on watching the inmate's behavior.

According to the psychiatrist, the best course of treatment is for the inmate to take what is known as an antipsychotic medication. But the inmate refuses to take such medication. He claims these drugs can produce serious—sometimes permanent—side effects and they make him feel "strange."

Outside the institution, people have a right to refuse treatment, including treatment for mental illness. But the state can overcome that right in certain circumstances and can put the person in a mental hospital and involuntarily medicate the person. But because civil commitment takes away a person's liberty and because of the seriousness of involuntarily medicating someone, due process requires that the decision to commit and medicate individuals against their will be approved by a court.

In early 1990, the Supreme Court looked at the question of whether similar due process protections were necessary to involuntarily medicate a mentally ill inmate in *Washington v. Harper*. The Court said a judicial hearing was not needed, but also said that "We have no doubt that (the inmate) possesses a significant liberty interest in avoiding the unwanted administration of antipsychotic drugs under the due process clause of the Fourteenth Amendment."[16]

Having decided that the decision to involuntarily medicate the inmate was protected by due process, the Court then indicated what sorts of circumstances would permit medicating the inmate and approved the procedures being followed by the State of Washington, where the case arose.

A person with a serious mental illness and who was dangerous to himself or herself or others may be medicated, when the treatment is in the inmate's medical interest, said the Court. The Court approved a hearing process for making these determinations, which somewhat resembled an inmate disciplinary hearing, although it included some greater procedural protections (the right to cross-examine witnesses, the right to be assisted by someone who understood the psychiatric issues involved, and a three-person hearing panel that included mental health experts). In 1992, the Supreme Court said that in certain circumstances pretrial detainees also could be involuntarily medicated.[17]

Substantive Due Process

In some situations, the focus of due process is on what is done, not just how it is done, which is the concern of procedural due process. Where the substance of the decision is the key issue, substantive due process or "fundamental fairness" will be the basis for the court's analysis. Under this approach, a court in essence may say, "It makes no difference how many procedural protections might accompany the decision or facts in question—what the government is doing simply should not be allowed, period."

The involuntary medication decision, *Washington v. Harper,* included a substantive due process component when the Court ruled on what sorts of circumstances had to exist to justify involuntarily medicating an inmate. Unless the inmate was dangerous to himself or others and involuntary treatment was in the inmate's medical interest, the inmate could not be involuntarily medicated, regardless of how many procedures the institution might go through.

But the main area in corrections where substantive due process is important is in litigation regarding the conditions of confinement of pretrial detainees. The Eighth Amendment's prohibition of cruel and unusual punishment regulates conditions of confinement for convicted persons. But the Eighth Amendment does not protect persons before they are convicted, such as pretrial detainees. To assure that conditions of confinement are at least no worse for pretrial detainees than for convicted persons, the courts review and regulate detainees' conditions of confinement under substantive due process. The end result is essentially the same: there is no clear difference between what conditions must exist for convicted persons (Eighth Amendment analysis) and for pretrial detainees (Fourteenth Amendment, substantive due process analysis). The difference really is only what legal route the court takes to the final result.

Substantive due process also may be the basis for a court reviewing allegations of excess force made by pretrial detainees

Equal Protection

It is sometimes said that equal protection outlaws discrimination between people or groups. This overstates the meaning of equal protection. The concept of equal protection says that groups of persons that are generally similar to one another should be treated the same by the government, unless the government can justify treating them differently.

The strength of the government's justification may have to be greater or lesser, depending on the groups and the reason for the discrimination between them. For instance, if discrimination on the basis of race (a so-called "suspect" classification) is shown (such as segregated cellblocks), the government must demonstrate a "compelling" need for the segregation. This is a very difficult burden to meet, so racial discrimination is almost never constitutionally justified. Con-scious decisions to discriminate on the basis of race are probably relatively rare. More likely, discrimination and resulting segregation of racial groups could occur as an unintentional consequence of applying a classification system.

Distinctions based on gender can be justified if they serve important government objectives and are substantially related to those objectives. This is a somewhat easier burden to meet than that for racial discrimination.

While there have been some racial segregation equal protection cases, these have been quite rare in recent years. Much more common have been cases which review differences between what is provided male versus female inmates.

Male Versus Female Facilities and Programs

It is common for facilities and programs provided for female inmates to be of lesser quality and quantity than those provided male inmates. An equal protection case asks (1) are there differences, and if so, then (2) what reasons might justify those differences?

For a number of years, courts looking at this issue would compare what was available for female inmates, program by program, to what was available for men. Where differences existed, corrections officials had to show that such discrimination against women had an "important purpose and that the relations between the purpose and the discrimination is substantial."[18] In equal protection parlance, this is known as the "intermediate scrutiny" test and is not an easy one for the government to meet.

Cases which found an equal protection violation generally would require improvements in the quality and quantity of what was available to women so that women's programs and facilities could be said to reflect "parity" with men's. That which was provided women should be "substantially equivalent to (that which was) provided to men, in other words, equivalent in substance if not form."[19]

Equal protection cases brought on behalf of women became known as "parity" cases. The approach taken in the parity cases (compare program by program, demand justification where differences were found) was generally accepted until the mid-1990s, when decisions from two courts of appeal cast doubt on whether the approach was proper.[20] These two decisions said that the way courts had been deciding that all women inmates easily could be compared to all or large groups of male inmates was improper and that while some groups of women properly may be compared to male inmates for equal protection purposes, large groups could not. The opinions also discredited the program-by-program comparison courts had been using.

Other courts of appeal may not follow the lead of these two decisions and instead may reaffirm the approach taken by the earlier "parity" cases. However, at the very least, what had been a fairly consistent trend in analyzing this type of case has been changed sharply in a way which, if followed by other courts, will make it much more difficult for female inmates to successfully sue over differences between their institutions and those of male inmates.

Review Questions

1. Why are there more procedural rights in a parole revocation hearing than a prison or jail disciplinary hearing?

2. What is the difference between procedural and substantive due process, and where might each arise in a prison or jail setting?

3. Under what circumstances may a hearing officer rely on evidence from a witness whose identity is not disclosed to the inmate charged with the offense?

Notes

1. *Washington v. Harper*, 494 U.S. 210 (1990).
2. *Hewitt v. Helms*, 459 U.S. 460 (1983).
3. *Burgin v. Nix*, 899 F.2d 733 (8th Circuit 1990).
4. 115 S.Ct. 2293 (1995).
5. 418 U.S. 539 (1974).

6. *Wolff v. McDonnell*; *Baxter v. Palmigiano*, 425 U.S. 308 (1976).
7. *Redding v. Fairman*, 717 F.2d 1105 (7th Cir., 1983).
8. *Sandin v. Conner*, 115 S.Ct. 2293 (1995).
9. *Whitford v. Boglino*, 63 F.3d 527 (7th Cir. 1995).
10. *Mitchell v. Dupnik*, 75 F.3d 517 (9th Cir. 1996).
11. *Baxter v. Palmigiano*, 425 U.S. 308 (1976).
12. *Wells v. Israel*, 629 F.Supp. 498 (E.D. Wisc., 1986); *McCollum v. Williford*, 793 F.2d 903 (7th Cir., 1986).
13. *Superintendent v. Hill*, 105 S.Ct. 2768 (1985).
14. In re *Reismiller*, 678 P.2d 323 (Wash., 1984).
15. In *Ponte v. Real*, 105 S.Ct. 2192 (1985), the Supreme Court said the justification for a witness denial need not be stated until an actual court challenge is made. However, prudence strongly suggests making a record of the justification at the time of the hearing. Waiting until the decision is taken to court prevents the decision from being reviewed and possibly corrected administratively (and thus preventing the suit altogether) and makes it likely that the hearing officer will be unable to remember why the witness was denied.
16. *Washington v. Harper*, 110 S.Ct. 1028 (1990).
17. *Riggins v. Nevada*, 112 S.Ct. 1810 (1992).
18. *Klinger v. Department of Corrections,* 31 F.3d 727, 737 (8th Cir., 1994), McMillan dissenting.
19. *Glover v. Johnson,* 478 F.Supp. 1075, 1079.
20. *Klinger.* supra. *Women Prisoners of the District of Columbia Department of Corrections*, 93 F.3d 910 (D.C. Cir., 1996).

XII.
The Correctional Employee and Litigation: How a Lawsuit Works

Being sued for actions arising out of the course of their employment is, unfortunately, an occupational hazard for persons working in corrections. While attorneys who defend these cases are familiar with how litigation "works," the defendant-employee often is not. This unfamiliarity may increase the anxiety attached to being sued. This chapter explains some of the mechanics of litigation, in the hopes that by understanding better what is going on in a case, the employee's litigation-related anxiety may be minimized.

Lawyers who defend suits obviously are very familiar with the way suits wind their way from summons and complaint through discovery and pretrial motions to trial, appeal, and final decision. Unfortunately, due to the press of work and because of their own uncertainty about what will happen next, the lawyer may forget to keep the client advised of progress of the suit or even if the case has been dismissed. (The overwhelming majority of cases filed directly by inmates are resolved in favor of defendants.)

The correctional employee who is a defendant in a suit should have no hesitation in asking his or her lawyer about the status of a case. It is the lawyer's obligation to keep the client advised of this information. So, if in doubt, ask.

Indemnification of Government Employees in Civil Actions

Among the first concerns of an employee working in a profession where lawsuits are so common often is, "Will I have to pay damages? Will I have to pay for my attorney?" The answer to these questions is generally "no."

State employees

Virtually every state in the country, by statutes often known as *tort claims* acts, has a procedure by which state employees sued in the line of work are (1) defended by the state attorney general and (2) indemnified for any costs of litigation, including attorneys' fees and damages. Even when a judgment may indicate it is against the defendant "personally," the state typically pays the judgment.

These defense/indemnification statutes act much like a private insurance policy for the employee. However, like many insurance policies, they are not absolute. While the exceptions vary from state to state, in general, the tort claims acts provide that the state is not under a duty to defend if the actions of the employee were outside the scope of the employee's duties or were not taken in good faith.

Thus, in one situation, a state refused to defend an employee of a women's prison in a suit that alleged he had fathered a child of the plaintiff, which was conceived and born while the woman was in the institution. After blood tests determined a very strong probability that the defendant in fact had fathered the child, the state withdrew its defense since there was no way impregnating an inmate could be seen as being within the duties of the defendant-officer.

Employees are wise to determine what exceptions or limitations may exist in defense/indemnification statutes in their jurisdiction and to determine if their state gives a broad or a narrow interpretation to what sort of actions may be within the "scope of employment." If the phrase is given a narrow, conservative interpretation, fewer suits against employees will be defended than if the phrase is given a broad interpretation.

Employees of local government

It is a little more difficult to generalize about the protections employees of local government enjoy in this area. Some states may have "little tort claims acts" that provide protection similar to that enjoyed by state employees. Other jurisdictions may carry insurance or self-insure. As with state employees, persons working for local government should determine the scope of protection they have from whatever insurance or statutory defense/indemnification procedure may exist in their jurisdiction.

Suits are serious matters and cannot be ignored by an employee named as a defendant. But the employee should not be greatly concerned that he or she will incur out-of-pocket expenses in defending the suit or in paying any judgment that the plaintiff might obtain.

Criminal Actions

In rare cases, criminal actions may be brought against government employees, either by state or federal prosecuting authorities. Defense of these actions by government attorneys, like defense of civil actions, also usually will depend on specific statutory authority. If such authority exists, it usually will be more restrictive than that for tort claims acts. In other words, there would be fewer situations in which the government could defend its employee in a job-related criminal action.

Summons and Complaint: The Beginnings of a Lawsuit

Generally speaking, the first notification a defendant has that a suit has been filed against him or her is with the receipt of two documents known as a summons and a complaint. The summons officially notifies the defendant that a suit has been filed and that the defendant has a limited period of time (usually twenty or thirty days) in which to respond to ("answer") the allegations of the complaint. The complaint indicates who the plaintiff and defendant are and states what the plaintiff alleges the defendant did or did not do, how that action or inaction violates the rights of the plaintiff, and what relief the plaintiff seeks.

Different courts have different means of "serving" a summons and complaint on a defendant. In some cases, the documents may be served by any disinterested person. Federal courts often require that a federal marshal serve the documents, although in some cases, service by certified mail is allowed. Generally, service by regular mail will not be considered effective, since the plaintiff ultimately may have to prove the summons and complaint were served on the defendant.

Employees should not attempt to decide whether service of documents that appear to be a summons and complaint (or other litigation-related documents) is good or not, but, instead, should notify their attorneys (or at least supervisors) immediately of the receipt of the documents. Prompt response to a summons and a complaint is necessary. Unless a formal answer or other appropriate documents are filed on behalf of the defendant within the time specified in the summons, a plaintiff, by proving the documents were served on the defendant, can obtain what is called a *default judgment* from the court. This judgment will award the plaintiff all, or at least a substantial part, of what the complaint asks for without any participation of the defendant whatsoever.

One thing a defendant served with a summons and a complaint should not do is answer the allegations personally by directly contacting either the plaintiff or the plaintiff's lawyer. The "answer" called for by the summons is a formal document that, unless properly prepared, may inadvertently hurt the defendant's defense of the suit in some way. The proper response to a summons and a complaint is for the defendant to contact his or her attorney. Agencies should have policies that address how an employee should notify the agency lawyer when served with a summons and a complaint.

What Next? Just the Facts, Ma'am

The lawyer defending the case will need to get the defendant's version of what happened soon after the complaint is served to be able to file an answer and to begin putting the defense of the case together. It is vital that the lawyer be advised of all the relevant facts surrounding the allegations. It is common for a complaint to allege facts that tend to support the claim of the lawsuit and to ignore or overlook facts not favorable to the plaintiff's position. Unless the defendant's lawyer is made aware of these facts, the case may be lost.

Sometimes a defendant will not tell the lawyer of certain facts because the defendant feels that they are not important or because they may be embarrassing to the individual. Again, withholding facts from the lawyer for these sorts of reasons can create very serious problems in the defense of the case.

Discovery

Under the rules by which suits operate (Rules of Civil Procedure), each side is entitled to attempt to find out virtually all of the facts possessed by the other side prior to the time the case goes to trial. This process is called *discovery*. The theory behind discovery is that cases will be settled more readily and justice will be served better when each side knows virtually all of the facts relevant to the suit. This is better than having the suit determined by surprise, when one side manages to hide key facts from the other until the trial is underway.

Discovery takes four primary forms: depositions, interrogatories, motions to produce documents, and requests for admissions. We will look at each of these.

Depositions

A deposition involves a lawyer for one side in a case examining a witness for the other side. The testimony is given under oath before a court reporter, but without a judge being present. Depositions of the plaintiff and defendants in suits are very common, and lawyers generally will attempt to depose any and all witnesses who the other side proposes to call at trial or other people who the lawyer feels may have information important to the case.

Interrogatories

Interrogatories are written questions from one side to the other, which the party is required to answer under oath. Interrogatories (often accompanied by requests for admissions to specific facts) generally look for fairly objective sorts of information, including such basic information as who the witnesses in a case may be.

Motions to produce

These are requests that the party produce documents in his or her possession that may be relevant to the suit. Motions to produce documents often accompany interrogatories. The interrogatory will ask the party to identify what documents may exist relevant to the controversy, and the motion to produce will request the identified documents be turned over to the requesting party.

Requests for admissions

Requests for admissions sometimes are used to determine basic facts in a case. They request the person to whom they are directed to either admit or deny a specific statement. Requests for admissions must be treated with care because the discovery rule that allows them requires that they be answered within a specific time (perhaps as little as twenty days) and provides that, unless a request for admission is denied or formally objected to within that time period, it will be treated as being admitted.

Handling discovery requests involves the cooperation of lawyer and client. The client should respond to discovery requests only through counsel, but the client may have to do the bulk of the work in responding since, for instance, the client (not the lawyer) will know what documents exist, where they are, and so forth.

Trial Avoidance Techniques

Trials often are avoided through an out-of-court settlement of the case. Some cases are dismissed before ever reaching the trial stage. There are two methods commonly used, especially in inmate-filed cases, that often result in dismissal of the case in favor of the defendant before trial.

Motions to dismiss

The first of these is known as a *motion* to *dismiss* or a *Rule 12(b)(6) motion* (which refers to the Rule of Civil Procedure that allows such motions). In a motion to dismiss, the defendant says, in essence, "Assuming all of the facts alleged by the plaintiff to be true, the plaintiff is still not entitled to any relief because the facts do not show the defendant violated any right of the plaintiff."

As an absurd example, an inmate-plaintiff might allege that his rights were violated because he was not allowed to bring a dozen friends from across the state to the prison at state expense to help him celebrate his birthday. A court would respond to a motion to dismiss in this case by saying, "Even if these facts are true, the state has no legal duty to spend money to help an inmate celebrate his birthday. Therefore, the plaintiff fails to state a claim upon which relief can be granted and the defendant's motion to dismiss is granted. Case dismissed."

Summary judgment

The second motion frequently used to dispose of cases before trial (and which can be brought by either party) is a motion for *summary judgment*. Here, where a party can show through affidavits and other documents that there are no significant facts at issue between the parties, the moving party is entitled to have the judge decide the case on its legal merits, in other words, grant a "summary" judgment. If there is no dispute about the material facts in a case, then there is no need to have a trial, and the judge can apply the law to the facts that the parties agree exist.

Summary judgments often are used in lawsuits in which the inmate claims that medical care he or she received was inadequate. Through affidavits of medical staff and copies of medical records, it can be shown what care the inmate actually received. A court then often will rule that the care the inmate received clearly showed more than "deliberate indifference to a serious medical need" and grant the defendants' motion for summary judgment.

Trial and Appeal

The trial is the process by which each side presents its case to the "trier of fact" (the judge or the jury) for determination as to whose version of the facts—the plaintiff's or the defendant's—is the more believable. In a jury case, the jury decides "the facts" but is instructed by the judge as to what the law is. The jury then determines if the facts that they have found violate the law as it is described to them.

Testifying

Where there is a trial, there is testimony. Testifying can be a very stressful process for a witness, especially when the witness may have important testimony to offer and is not familiar with the process of testifying from other court appearances.

Prior to going onto the witness stand, the lawyer presenting the witness should discuss the issues that will be covered and the questions to be asked with the witness. There is nothing wrong with this, and, in fact, no good lawyer will put witnesses on the stand without talking to them. (A saying among lawyers is, "Never ask a witness a question unless you know the answer.") If asked by the opposing lawyer, "Have you discussed your testimony with anyone prior to taking the stand?," the witness should not hesitate in saying, "Yes." If asked with whom the testimony was discussed, the witness can readily state it was with his or her lawyer.

There are many lists of suggestions for witnesses. The following list may help the witness present testimony in the best possible way.

1. Be familiar with the subject of your testimony before taking the stand. Review your records and notes. Review depositions you gave, perhaps months before trial.

2. Dress neatly. Act and appear professional the entire time you are at court, not just while you are on the witness stand. If you wear a uniform, check with your lawyer as to whether you should wear the uniform to testify.

3. Arrive early and let your lawyer know you are present. You may have to wait outside the courtroom before testifying.

4. Do not memorize your testimony. Not only will it not sound natural if you forget your "lines," but your testimony will be very unconvincing.

5. When testifying, speak loudly and clearly. Speak so that you can be heard by the farthest juror. And speak. You cannot answer with a nod or shake of the head or a shrug. Your testimony is being transcribed, and the court reporter only can record verbal answers, not body language.

6. Listen to the question. Be sure you understand it before answering, and answer only the question asked. Think about your answer before you give it, and avoid giving snap answers. If you do not understand the question, ask that it be clarified.

7. Do not volunteer additional information. If you feel you have answered the question, stop talking. If the lawyer delays in asking the next question, do not feel obligated to fill the silence with an additional answer.

8. Try to answer questions "yes" or "no" or otherwise with short answers. If the lawyer wants only a yes or no answer and you cannot answer with just a yes or no, say so. You should be allowed to explain your answer.

9. Correct answers that you give in error. It is easier to correct a mistake as it happens than to try to fix it later.

10. Witnesses normally will not be allowed to give opinions. Testify just as to the facts, and do not be afraid to say "I do not know" or "I cannot remember." Do not exaggerate or try to make up details in an attempt to make your testimony sound better. Stick to what you know. TELL THE TRUTH! Telling the truth, and the whole truth begins when you first talk to a lawyer.

11. Always be courteous. This may be easier said than done if the lawyer questioning you is hostile. But getting angry with the lawyer or trying to act "smart" with the lawyer usually will work against you.

12. Do not look to the court for help or guidance in answering a question. Your lawyer should object if the question is improper. If no objection is made, you should answer the question. An exception to this is where you are testifying without a lawyer (perhaps introducing records in a dispute between two other parties). In this situation, you may ask the judge about answering, at least to a limited degree.

13. Stop talking when the judge interrupts or an attorney objects to a question. When being cross-examined by the opposing lawyer, it is a good practice to pause for a couple of seconds before beginning your answer to allow your lawyer to make objections.

14. When your testimony is complete, leave the courtroom with a confident expression. Normally, you should not linger in the courtroom (unless you are a party in the case and attending the entire trial).

Trial and your lawyer

While to the observer, a trial may seem to be a slow, plodding activity, to the lawyer actually trying the case, the trial is a very intense time. The court expects one witness to be called after another and the lawyer is expected to be ready to proceed with the case from start to finish without delay. While a witness worries about his or her own testimony, the lawyer may be worrying about testimony and scheduling of a dozen witnesses, plus a variety of other concerns.

Because of the intensity of the trial and because of the pressure to keep the trial moving, an individual witness may feel he or she is being treated brusquely by the court and even by the lawyer who called the witness. To a large extent, this is simply inevitable, and the witness should not expect to have time to discuss the testimony with the lawyer just before or after the witness is called to testify. However, a good lawyer will make every effort to discuss the testimony with a witness at some time shortly before the witness testifies.

Appeal

On appeal, no further testimony is taken. Instead, the appellate court reviews the written record from the trial and determines if the law was correctly applied. Except in rare cases, the appellate court is bound by the facts found by the original judge or jury, since the appellate court is not able to evaluate the credibility and demeanor of the witnesses who testified at trial.

Conclusion

The correctional employee should remember that, except in truly rare circumstances, lawsuits against an employee do not threaten the employee's personal finances. Additionally, although offenders may file a large number of suits, the overwhelming majority of such suits are resolved in favor of the defendant/correctional employee, usually without even going to trial.

It is equally important to recognize that suits are serious matters and should not be taken lightly. The employee who is sued needs to make prompt contact with legal counsel and work closely with counsel through the defense of the case.

Review Questions

1. Under what circumstances is an agency likely to refuse to defend an employee sued by an inmate?

2. Name two types of discovery.

3. True or false: When testifying, the witness should try to memorize answers to the lawyers' questions.

XIII.
Officers' Rights

Inmates are not the only people to repeatedly turn to the courts to settle disputes in the last quarter of the twentieth century. Americans of every description are becoming quick to file lawsuits. America is a litigious society.

Corrections has not escaped being the target of lawsuits from persons other than inmates, and officers may see these suits during their work. In some cases, officers may file such claims and/or be the target of them.

Sources of Officers' Rights

Correctional staff are increasingly sensitive about their rights and the obligations of others toward officers. While inmates usually must look to the Constitution for legal protection, legally enforceable rights of staff come from many sources, not just the Constitution.

Union contracts

Where a union exists, the labor agreement may create a variety of rights for union members. These can include seniority and job assignments, overall working conditions, procedures to be followed in discipline, grievance procedures, layoffs, and other protections. An employer's ability to implement a urine testing program (which may include random testing) may be limited by the bargaining agreement—the employer may not have the power to begin a urinalysis program without the agreement of the union.

Where collective bargaining between an agency and employees is permitted, it is controlled by state law. The state law will define what subjects are open for collective bargaining and what are not. Bargainable issues typically include such things as working conditions and other personnel-related matters. Workload and safety generally are

159

considered to be mandatory subjects of bargaining. Nonbargainable issues are those that are considered to be managerial.

Unfortunately, the line between subjects that are or are not subject to bargaining often is not clear. Two issues that often are subject to dispute as to whether they are bargainable issues are employee urine testing programs and the decision to make a workplace smoke-free.

Civil service laws

At the very least, laws and regulations adopted under civil service laws usually define the procedures to be followed in employee discipline proceedings, defining the due process owed the employee facing discipline. Many correctional administrators complain that the often stringent legal requirements created by these laws (and sometimes by union contracts, as well) make it very difficult to discipline an employee.

Discrimination laws

Statutes and regulations have been adopted at both the federal and state level prohibiting discrimination against a variety of protected groups or categories. Discrimination on the basis of race, sex, national origin, religion, color, age, and handicap generally are prohibited. Discrimination issues may arise in a variety of employment-related contexts, beginning with job advertising and recruiting; and continuing through testing; hiring; making assignments; transferring; promoting; training; disciplining; providing compensation and benefits; terminating; and virtually every other term, condition, and privilege of employment.

Discrimination claims may be brought by specific individuals or by groups claiming they have been systematically discriminated against in some way. In one case, an employer who passed over a woman for a major promotion in a large accounting firm told her she should be "more feminine" in a number of ways. Standing alone, this sort of sexual stereotyping would have violated the law and not been a legitimate ground for denying her a promotion. But the employer claimed it had other legally permissible reasons for passing over the woman. The Supreme Court said that where first the employee shows that gender was a motivating factor for the decision, the employer still could escape liability by proving by a preponderance of the evidence (a lower "burden of proof" than the lower court had required) that it would have reached the same employment decision ("We wouldn't have promoted her anyway.")[1]

This shows the legal complexity that can arise in a case involving a single person. The complexity multiplies overwhelmingly when a group claims it has been discriminated against. The evidence in such cases seldom will be direct. An employer will not have a written policy that says, "We don't promote women or minorities." The evidence in such cases often is statistical: the number of protected group members in a given employment category is so small it only can be explained by discrimination. The Supreme Court has approved such statistical approaches, saying an inference of discrimination may be drawn through such means, but the comparison (in a promotional case situation) must be between the number of higher level jobs and the numbers of the protected group in the labor market qualified to hold those jobs. The employees also must show a particular employment practice that causes a statistical disparity. Where the employees meet these difficult burdens, the employer may defend itself successfully by showing the challenged practice serves legitimate employment goals.[2]

The area of discrimination law becomes even more complicated because most claims arise under laws passed by Congress or state legislatures and later are interpreted by the courts. A court may interpret a law in a way not intended by the legislative body that passed it. This may lead the legislative body to pass amendments to the law to correct what it feels was the court's misapplication of the legislative intent.

Affirmative action

In a sense, affirmative action programs are the flip side of discrimination laws. The general goal of these programs is to increase the number of protected group members in the workforce. But unless carefully structured and implemented, affirmative action programs can discriminate illegally against other people. A voluntary affirmative action plan that includes goals, not specific quotas, and is designed to attain, not maintain, a balanced workforce, is acceptable if it is attempting to remedy a "manifest imbalance" in a "traditionally segregated job category."[3] The imbalance sought to be corrected need not be the result of actions by the employer, but can be the result of societal pressures and attitudes. But where there is a specific history of an employer discriminating against a protected group, specific hiring quotas may be ordered by a court.[4]

Sexual Discrimination and Harassment

One form of unlawful discrimination warrants special discussion. Sexual discrimination is outlawed by Title VII of the federal Civil Rights Act, 42 USC 2000e. Because increasing numbers of women are entering the workforce in male facilities where the workforce traditionally has been almost all male, sexual discrimination can be a very real problem in such workplaces.

Unless there is a truly legitimate reason for treating persons differently on the basis of their sex (a "bona fide occupational qualification" or BFOQ), discrimination is illegal. The same exception applies to types of generally unlawful discrimination, such as racial discrimination. The BFOQ concept is narrowly defined and applied. One example where it might be applied is to justify a single-sex post in an institution where the post (or a specific task) involved very close scrutiny of inmates in states of undress. In this situation, use of officers of the opposite sex of the inmates would be seen as an invasion of the inmates' privacy rights.

While sexual discrimination may be thought of as only including such things as refusing persons a job because of their sex, the concept also includes sexual harassment. And it is sexual harassment that may present the most potential conflict in the male prison setting.

Sexual harassment must involve one or more of the following conditions:

1. Submission to the conduct is made (either directly or by inference) a condition of employment or for other employment-related decisions (promotions, working conditions, and so forth). The most flagrant example of this exists where an employer or supervisor tells someone, "If you want this job, you must have sex with me."
2. The conduct has either the purpose or the effect of unreasonably interfering with a person's work performance or creating an intimidating, hostile, or offensive work environment. This is probably the most common area of complaint. (A hostile

work environment also can be the basis for a claim of racial discrimination.)

Under the "hostile work environment" approach, such things as unwanted touches, comments, or photos (physical, verbal, or visual conduct) may create the basis of a legitimate complaint. Sexual stereotyping (such as asking a female employee to get coffee, take notes, and do other "women's work") also can create a hostile work environment.

In general, the conduct must be unwanted, and the persons who feel offended by the conduct must make it known that they want the conduct to stop. This can add a level of uncertainty because milder forms of potentially sexually harassing conduct may be seen by some as routine and not offensive, but may be very offensive to others.

Employees should receive training on sexual harassment and discrimination issues. The following basic points should be remembered:

1. Sexual harassment is against the law.
2. Sexual harassment suits can be very expensive and time-consuming to defend and can result in liability both against individual staff members and the agency.
3. Sexual harassment suits can be very destructive of employee morale, as one group becomes pitted against another.
4. Inmates will be quick to sense the disruption among staff and try to exploit it.

Rights for Disabled Staff

The Americans with Disabilities Act (ADA) prohibits discrimination against otherwise qualified staff or job applicants on the basis of a disability. The law requires the employer to make "reasonable accommodations" for disabled persons and includes various remedies, including lawsuits for people who feel their rights under the law have been violated. Compliance with the requirements of ADA in the hiring and employment process may require not only various physical changes in buildings, but changes in employment testing, job qualifications, and job structure. The ADA is discussed at greater length in Chapter XV.

Workplace Safety

Workplace safety is increasingly a "legal issue." Here, claims may arise under union contracts, under state or federal occupational safety and health laws, or under the Constitution. In one startling action, correctional officers and their union joined with inmates in 1989 to file a lawsuit against a large metropolitan jail challenging crowding and the alleged lack of workplace safety (argued to be a by-product of the crowding).[5]

Other constitutional claims made by correctional staff about inadequate safety have not done well in court. According to at least two federal appeals courts, the state has no constitutional duty to protect officers. Since such a duty exists for inmates, why not for officers? The courts said it is because the officers are free to leave. The duty to protect applies only to those held in the state's custody. "The state must protect those it throws into snake pits, but the state need not guarantee that volunteer snake charmers will not be bitten," said one court.[6]

If the state has no constitutional duty to provide a safe workplace, it does have such a duty under occupational safety and health laws and regulations, which may be enforced either by federal or state agencies. Under the federal Occupational Safety and Health Act (OSHA), an employer has the general duty to keep the workplace free of recognized hazards that are likely to cause death or serious injury. Many states have similar laws.

In Oregon, the corrections department was fined by the state's accident prevention division for inadequately training correctional officers and not providing enough armed help for them in emergencies. In Washington state, the corrections department was ordered to provide bulletproof vests for parole officers.[7]

While a safety-related complaint made to a state regulatory agency may not be as dramatic as filing a lawsuit in federal court, these agencies may prove to be a faster, more effective remedy than federal court.

Environmental Issues

Correctional facilities, like other public and private enterprises, must comply with the various local, state, and federal environmental laws and regulations that have been adopted over the last several years. These include writing environmental impact statements for new institutions, handling litigation over the siting of new facilities (which may be opposed by people on environmental grounds as well as on other grounds), disposing of sewage and garbage, water usage and water quality, and a variety of other issues.

Environmental legal issues may or may not affect officers directly. In some cases, they directly may involve safety in the workplace, such as where an agency is required to remove asbestos from an institution. Other situations, such as where a facility can be located and what it must do to comply with sewage disposal rules, may be decided before a facility is built or has staff.

Other Statutory Rights

Various other federal laws include protections for correctional employees. Among these are the Fair Labor Standards Act (FLSA) and the Family Medical Leave Act (FMLA).

The Fair Labor Standards Act deals primarily with when an employer must pay overtime. The statute and accompanying regulations adopted by the U.S. Department of Labor are very complex. The basic principle of the law is that an employee is entitled to overtime pay (one and a half times regular pay) whenever the employee works more than forty hours per week. In some circumstances, compensatory time may be given instead of overtime pay. For most correctional officers, the need for overtime is not computed on the basis of a forty-hour work week, but instead by looking at hours worked over a longer work period, which may range from seven to twenty-eight days.

The Family Medical Leave Act generally gives employees the right to take leave (which may be unpaid) for medical reasons, for the birth or adoption of a child, and to care for a sick spouse, child, or parent. As with the Fair Labor Standards Act, this is a complicated law, with a variety of limitations and restrictions.

Privacy Issues

In Chapter VII, we examined the rights of inmates to be free from unreasonable searches and seizures. The right comes from the Fourth Amendment. Officers also are protected by the Fourth Amendment, and the courts will take the same approach to analyzing an officer's search case as is used in an inmate's search case: The court will balance the needs of the institution for the particular type of search against the reasonable expectations of privacy that the officer enjoys.

In general, the officer enjoys a greater expectation of privacy than does the inmate. But this expectation is not as great as it would be outside the institution. By choosing to work in a setting where security is very important, the officer's rights under the Fourth Amendment are reduced somewhat from what they would be on the street.

As long as searches are for work-related, administrative purposes (and not for criminal purposes), the Fourth Amendment's normal requirements of probable cause and search warrants do not apply to employment searches. Depending on the justification for the search and its intrusion, such work-related searches may require reasonable suspicion or, in some cases, may be done randomly.[8]

Thus, the institution may search purses and briefcases of staff coming into the facility, may pat search staff, and require them to pass magnetometer searches without any specific cause or suspicion. But the institution must have reasonable suspicion to require the officer to submit to a strip search. Officer's vehicles may be subject to search, at least if they are parked on institution grounds where inmates would have access to them.[9]

To some extent, institution rules and policies are relevant in deciding if an employee has a reasonable expectation of privacy that might limit the types of searches the institution may be able to conduct legally. For instance, if institution rules and practices clearly indicate lockers are subject to search without cause, a court is more likely to approve random locker searches than if the employees are given the impression both through policy and actual practice that their lockers are their own property and not subject to search absent some level of cause.

Random urine testing

The combination of increased drug usage among the general public and the development of reliable means of urine testing for drugs produced controversy and litigation during the 1980s. For staff, the question was under what circumstances, if any, an employer could randomly test employees or job applicants for drug usage.

The Supreme Court decided two cases in 1989 that said that in at least some circumstances, urine testing could be done without any particularized cause or suspicion that the employee had been using drugs.[10] From these cases, other courts now generally have ruled that random testing of employees whose jobs are particularly concerned with such things as public safety may be required without violating the Fourth Amendment. Correctional officers who have direct contact with inmates are among those courts have approved for random testing.[11] Although testing itself has been approved, there still may be concerns with such issues as the amount of privacy afforded the officer when actually providing the urine sample. Labor agreements may limit an employer's ability to implement a urine testing program, since the program may be something that must be bargained for with the union.

A 1988 survey by the National Institute of Justice showed nineteen state prison systems and the Federal Bureau of Prisons had employee drug testing programs, and only one of these used random testing for permanent employees. In the random testing program, every Monday twenty names of employees at the Georgia State Prison are drawn from a box, and those employees are given a urine test. (The warden's name goes in the box along with every other employee.) When begun in 1984, approximately 40 percent of the employees tested were positive. By 1988, this figure had dropped to about 10 percent. This reduction also was accompanied by a sharp reduction in the amount of contraband drugs in the prison.[12] Employees who test positive are fired. But employees who admit a drug problem and seek assistance through an Employee Assistance Program before they test positive are retained.

Polygraph Tests

Federal law and regulations impose strict limitations on the use of polygraphs (lie detector tests) by private sector employers, but do not limit use of polygraphs by public sector employers such as state or local governments. However, many states have laws restricting or sometimes prohibiting the use of lie detectors. Even if the use of a polygraph might not violate the Constitution, it easily could violate state law. A Maryland jury awarded $900,000 in compensatory damages plus $4.1 million in punitive damages to four employees who were wrongfully fired for refusing to take a polygraph test.[13]

Even where state law permits an employer to require an employee to take a polygraph examination, courts may prohibit use of the results in either an administrative hearing or in a court proceeding.

Use of polygraphs as well as other sometimes controversial means of testing are sometimes used in screening applicants for correctional

167

jobs. Since correctional employers, like other employers, are sued from time to time by someone claiming to have been injured in some way by an employee the employer negligently hired, it is easy to understand why many employers are using an increased number of tools to try to screen prospective employees very carefully.

In a 1988 decision, the Third Circuit Court of Appeals refused to find that a polygraph test for prospective correctional employees violated either the due process or equal protection rights of the would-be employees.[14] The court made its decision less on a belief that the polygraph was highly accurate than because it could find no constitutional interest the job applicants had in the jobs for which they were applying. So, while polygraph results may not be used as part of the evidence to fire someone, they may be used as part of the decision to hire the person in the first place. Agency personnel policies should address under what circumstances, if at all, an employee or prospective employee may be required to take a polygraph test.

Confidential information

An employer may be able to obtain a substantial amount of personal information about an employee. This might include information such as drug usage, medical conditions, prior criminal history, participation in counseling, and so forth. While the employer may have a legitimate reason for knowing this confidential information, that does not entitle the employer to release that information to people who have no reason to know it. This can include not only release to the general public, but also release to other employees.

Where private facts about an employee are improperly released, the employee may be able to successfully sue for invasion of privacy. In general, when an employer has information the reasonable person would consider private, the employer should have a legitimate business reason for disclosing that information even within the organization. Protecting confidential information becomes particularly important when the information could be particularly embarrassing and potentially damaging to the employee. This would include information about an employee's drug use and about employees who might be carriers of the AIDS virus or even have AIDS.

Due Process and Employee Discipline

For many years, it was assumed that the typical civil service employee disciplinary hearing provided all the due process necessary to terminate an employee. Usually these procedures included a full hearing, which occurred sometime after the employee actually was terminated. If the employee won the hearing, the relief could include not only reinstatement but also payment of lost wages.

In 1985, the Supreme Court looked at the question of what sort of due process protections the government employee had and whether a post-termination hearing under state civil service laws was sufficient. In the case of *Cleveland Board of Education v. Loudermill*,[15] the Court decided a post-termination hearing alone did not provide the employee with due process. Instead, the Fourteenth Amendment required a limited pretermination hearing in addition to whatever hearing rights the employee might have after the termination.

The pretermination hearing, the Court said, is not to resolve the propriety of the decision to fire the employee. It is only to serve as a check against mistakes and to decide if there are reasonable grounds to believe the charges against the employee are true. Therefore, the hearing required by the *Loudermill* case is quite simple and informal. The employee must be given either written or oral notice of the charges. The employer must give an explanation of the evidence against the employee, who must have a chance to present his or her side of the case.

Conclusion

When employees feel their concerns and problems are not being addressed adequately by the employer, they increasingly are willing to take those concerns to court. In contrast to inmates, who are largely limited to raising claims under the Constitution, there are several different legal vehicles that employees may use to protect and advance their interests.

Review Questions

1. List three sources of officers' rights.

2. True or false: While sexual discrimination is against the law, sexual harassment is not.

3. True or false: Courts consistently have ruled that random urine testing of correctional officers is an unreasonable search.

Notes

1. *Price Waterhouse v. Hopkins*, 109 S.Ct. 1775 (1989).
2. *Ward's Cove Packing v. Atonio*, 109 S.Ct. 2115 (1989).
3. *Johnson v. Transportation Agency*, Santa Clara County, 107 S.Ct. 1442 (1987).
4. *U.S. v. Paradise*, 107 S.Ct. 1053 (1987).
5. *Hammer v. King County*, W.D. No. C89-521R.
6. *Walker v. Rowe*, 791 F.2d 507, 511 (7th Cir., 1986). *Washington v. District of Columbia*, 802 F.2d 1478 (D.C. Cir., 1986).
7. Collins. *Correctional Law*. 1987, p. 109.
8. *O'Connor v. Ortega*, 107 S.Ct. 1492 (1987).
9. *McDonnell v. Hunter* 809 F.2d 1302 (8th Cir., 1987).
10. *Skinner v. Railway Labor Executives' Association*, 109 S.Ct. 1402 (1989), *National Treasury Employees Union v. Von Raab*, 109 S.Ct. 1378 (1989).
11. *Taylor v. O'Grady*, 888 F.2d 1189 (7th Cir., 1989).
12. *Employee Drug-testing Policies in Prison Systems*, National Institute of Justice Research in Action, August 1988.
13. *Monlodis v. Cook*, 494 A.2d 212 (Md. Ct. Spec. App., 1984).
14. *Anderson v. City of Philadelphia*, 845 F.2d 1216 (3rd Cir., 1988).
15. 105 S.Ct. 1487 (1985).

XIV.
AIDS

AIDS (Acquired Immune Deficiency Syndrome) remains a continuing source of controversy and concern in American society, generally, and in corrections in particular. While there have been a substantial number of lawsuits decided that deal with AIDS in correctional institutions, courts have not become as involved in imposing requirements for dealing with HIV issues as many assumed when HIV first emerged in the corrections scene in the mid-1980s.[1]

Most court decisions regarding AIDS and inmates tend to favor deferring to the judgment of correctional administrators. With some exceptions, courts have tended to leave AIDS issues to the policy judgment of administrators instead of turning them into legal mandates.

Segregation and Testing

One of the more common issues about AIDS is whether inmates who are known to be positive for the HIV virus *must* be segregated to protect the rest of the population, *may* be segregated, or must be allowed to remain in the general population unless other grounds exist to segregate them. In what is probably the leading case dealing with segregation of HIV-positive inmates (*Harris v. Thigpen*), the Eleventh Circuit Court of Appeals said that a policy of segregating all inmates known to be HIV-positive did not violate the constitutional rights of those segregated.[2] This case also approved a policy of testing all inmates to determine if they were HIV-positive. By contrast, another appeals court said that a mandatory testing policy could not be justified on the basis of the conclusory assertion that testing furthered a legitimate penological interest.[3] Officials had to be more specific as to what interest (such as security or health) was being furthered by the testing policy and how that interest was furthered.

Courts seem to be taking a neutral position on some AIDS issues. While the *Harris* decision approved a mandatory testing policy, another court said that the decision not to test all inmates for HIV and to try to integrate HIV-positive inmates into the general population did not show deliberate indifference to the interests of non-HIV-positive inmates.[4]

While the *Harris* decision said that the Constitution did not prohibit the segregation of all HIV-positive inmates, the court also said that a federal statute, the Rehabilitation Act, would allow segregation only after an individual consideration as to whether the HIV-positive inmate was "otherwise qualified" to participate in particular institution programs. The same individualized determination would be required under the Americans with Disabilities Act (ADA), since it includes HIV status as a "disability" and generally requires that people with disabilities who are otherwise qualified to participate in a government service, activity, or program be allowed to participate unless the government can meet a very difficult burden to justify discriminating against persons because of their disability.

Eight years after holding that the Rehabilitation Act applied to inmates, the Eleventh Circuit held that the Act afforded no relief to them. The Act contains an exception—it does not prevent discriminating against someone on the basis of a disability if "by reason of . . . disease or infection, [a person] would constitute a direct threat to the health or safety of other individuals." 20 USC § 705(20)(D). The court felt that HIV-positive prison inmates fell into this exception. The court felt that the only way to accommodate the risk of placing HIV-positive inmates in programs with other inmates would be to add more staff and that this would create an unreasonable hardship on the department of corrections. This decision is a very conservative one. Alabama remains virtually alone in its decision to segregate all HIV-positive inmates.

The ADA probably will make it virtually impossible to segregate all HIV-positive inmates automatically and thereby cut off their access to programs and services available to the general population. Segregation or other limits on program participation may be approved in individual, extraordinary cases.

> ## Case Study: Officer's Failure to Protect Nurse Results in Huge Damage Award
>
> Although testimony was contradictory, the trial court found the following facts: The inmate was in the hospital. The two officers assigned from the prison to guard the inmate probably knew the inmate was HIV-positive. The inmate, who weighed less than 125 pounds, tore off his oxygen mask and disconnected his IV tube. A relatively long struggle with several nurses ensued, at least partially related to a seizure the inmate had.
>
> Although the nurses made requests and then adamant demands for the officers to intervene and restrain the inmate, the officers never came to the nurses' help. During the struggle with the inmate, one nurse was holding the IV needle that had come out of the inmate's arm. She was bumped and accidentally stuck the needle into the hand of one of the other nurses. As a result of the needle stick, the second nurse became HIV-positive.
>
> The court held that the officers were negligent in failing to come to the aid of the nurses and awarded $5.4 million damages, the award to be paid by the state of New York. On appeal, the damages were raised to $6.1 million, *Doe v. New York State*, 595 N.Y.S. 2d 592 (1993). It is not clear why the officers did not intervene. The case does show the amount of damages that can be assessed in such cases.

Disclosure

Probably the AIDS issues that are the most serious but that also are not clearly resolved are those relating to disclosure of AIDS information and medical care. Who should be told an inmate is HIV-positive? Should all inmates be tested and the test results disclosed to staff?

Many custody officers feel very strongly that they have a right to know whether those who they supervise might be carrying the HIV virus and could have the potential for transmitting AIDS. Others argue that AIDS is very difficult to catch or transmit and that AIDS cannot be caught through casual contact between the carrier and another person.

They argue that if staff practice "universal precautions" around blood (treat all blood as though it might carry the HIV virus), staff will be safe and therefore need not know which inmates actually carry the virus. They also argue that if staff generally know who has the HIV virus, that fact will be common knowledge, and the HIV carrier could be in danger as a result of that disclosure to people who clearly have no need to know (such as other inmates).

State laws and regulations often speak specifically to disclosure (or confidentiality) of AIDS information, sometimes making such information highly confidential and imposing penalties on people for improper disclosure. Courts also have ruled that improper disclosure can be an invasion of privacy and entitle the person to damages. For instance, one court allowed a case to go forward that claimed that prison medical staff had casually and without any medical or treatment purpose discussed an inmate's positive AIDS test with nonmedical staff and other inmates.[6] In another case, the wife and children of a man who had AIDS successfully sued a police department for improperly disclosing the fact that the man had AIDS to a neighbor, who in turn contacted the school and the media claiming the children might have AIDS.[7]

Yet even by 1999, courts were unclear on what constitutional limitations, if any, existed on disclosure of an inmate's HIV status. However, a trend appears to be developing in favor of at least limited disclosure. At least two circuits have suggested that disclosure of HIV status may be permissible in situations where the disclosure furthers a legitimate interest of the government.[8] However, the *Anderson* case cited in the footnote also speculates that if the disclosure were done out of a punitive motive, it could violate the inmate's rights under the Eighth Amendment. In both of the cited cases, the disclosure over which the inmate sued was not done in accordance with an agency policy, but was done casually. In each case, the court said that the employee was entitled to qualified immunity, as the law was not "clearly established" regarding disclosure of an inmate's HIV status.

The Prison Litigation Reform Act (PLRA) prevented one court from evaluating a privacy claim brought by an HIV-positive inmate. The inmate claimed an officer improperly broke into his sealed medical records and disclosed the fact that the inmate was dying of AIDS. But the claim ran afoul of the PLRA's provision that an inmate cannot bring a claim for emotional or mental injury "without a prior showing of physical injury" 42 U.S.C. § 1997e(e). The inmate's claim sought damages based on emotional injury he said he suffered because of the wrongful disclosure. The court upheld the constitutionality of the PLRA provision, applied it to the case, and agreed with the lower court that the claim was barred. The case was dismissed[9]

While courts have not yet drawn clear lines for corrections as to who may or may not receive information about the HIV status of an inmate, it is clear that this remains a potentially volatile area of the law. Even if courts eventually decide that disclosure of HIV status to officers is permissible, what about disclosure to inmates or to persons outside the prison?

Because disclosure issues may involve very sensitive areas of law where there is not yet clear guidance from the courts, it is very important for staff to recognize that HIV information is generally confidential. Following agency policy on HIV disclosure will be important. Where anyone, inmate or staff, who is HIV-positive is injured in some way (including reputation in the community) because institution staff revealed that the person was HIV-positive, the burden will be on those who made the disclosure to justify it as being necessary to further some legitimate interest of the institution. Even if a court decides disclosure of an inmate's HIV status does not violate a constitutional right of the inmate, the officer making such a disclosure could face disciplinary charges for violating agency policy or face a suit under state law.

Medical Care

There is no question that AIDS is a serious medical need and that inmates who suffer from the disease have a right to be treated. Treating an AIDS patient can cost thousands of dollars per year. At least one court has assumed that treatment with AZT, a drug that can delay the onset of AIDS, reduce the symptoms of AIDS, and prolong the life of the AIDS sufferer, is constitutionally necessary.[10] Under the "deliberate indifference to serious medical needs" test for evaluating the adequacy of prison or jail medical care (*see* Chapter VIII), AIDS is clearly a "serious medical need." It is difficult to see how denying someone medications that would substantially prolong the person's life and would ease the symptoms of a dreadful disease would not be "deliberate indifference."

It is an interesting comment on American society that inmates in correctional facilities can obtain medical care as a matter of right that is not available to the general public. This disparity is not new, but is highlighted in the AIDS area, as one hears of people committing criminal acts in order to obtain AIDS treatment that is either not available to them in the community or too expensive for them to afford.

Staff and AIDS

In addition to the staff concern about testing and disclosure of AIDS information about inmates, there are also serious concerns about the extent to which an agency can test employees or take adverse action (such as termination) against an employee who the agency knows to be HIV-positive.

Since being HIV-positive (not even necessarily having begun to develop symptoms of AIDS) is a disability protected by the ADA and since ADA protects employees, automatically discharging an employee because of his or her HIV status is illegal. To support discharging such an employee, the employer will have to demonstrate that the employee cannot perform the essential functions of the job, with or without some reasonable accommodation. Labor law authorities recommend against testing employees or job applicants for AIDS, even if state law would permit such testing.[11]

Should an employer obtain information showing an employee was HIV-positive, the information should be handled with the utmost confidentiality, given the strong public stigma and often hysteria that accompanies HIV information.

AIDS and Training

After several years of being in the news almost constantly, AIDS remains a frightening disease that is not clearly understood by many people. Public hysteria remains about AIDS. Because of the fear many people have, it is possible for them to overreact and out of ignorance take action against someone suspected of carrying the AIDS virus. When this sort of action occurs in a correctional facility, it clearly could violate the rights of the individual, be that person an inmate or staff member.

Therefore, it is very important that both staff and inmates receive training about what AIDS is and what it is not. Understanding the disease will reduce the possibility of taking inappropriate action out of ignorance.

Notes

1. For a general discussion of AIDS and corrections, see *AIDS in Correctional Facilities*: *Issues and Options*, a series of books and shorter materials from the National Institute of Justice written by Dr. Theodore Hammett. These volumes provide a great deal of data and other information about AIDS generally and its prevalence in correctional facilities.
2. *Harris v. Thigpen*, 941 F.2d 1495 (1th Cir., 1991).
3. *Walker v. Sumner*, 917 F.2d 382 (9th Cir., 1990).
4. *Portee v. Tollison*, 753 F.Supp. 184 (D. SC, 1990), aff'd. 929 F.2d 694 (4th Cir., 1991).
5. *Onishea v. Hopper*, 171 F.3d 1289 (11th Cir., 1999). This is the same case as *Harris*, note 2. The names of the parties changed.
6. *Woods v. White*, 689 F.Supp. 874 (W.D. Wisc., 1988). *See* Cohen, *Aids: Confidentiality and Disclosure, 1 Correctional Law Reporter*. 17. 1989.
7. *Doe v. Barrington*, 729 F.Supp. 376 (D. N.J., 1990).
8. *Powell v. Schriver*, 175 F.3d 107 (2d Cir., 1999), *Anderson v. Romero*, 72 F.3d 518, 525 (7th Cir.1995).
9. *Davis v. District of Columbia*, 158 F.3d 1342 (D.C. Cir., 1998).
10. *Nolley v. Erie County*, 776 F.Supp. 715 (W.D. N.Y, 1992).
11. Kahn, Brown, Sepke and Lanzarone. 1990. *Personnel Director's Legal Guide*, 2d ed., Warren, Gorham and Lamont. p. 9-29.

XV.

The Americans with Disabilities Act

In 1990, Congress passed the Americans with Disabilities Act (ADA). This law, described as the "Bill of Rights" for the disabled, prohibits discrimination against people with disabilities in employment, public services and transportation, public accommodations, and telecommunications.

For purposes of those working in corrections, there are two major sections of the ADA which are of major importance. Title I provides protections for persons seeking employment or actually working in corrections. Title II provides protections to persons who are applicants for or recipients of government services or programs. The group protected by Title II includes inmates and visitors to correctional facilities, among others.

The Supreme Court has decided two cases regarding the ADA, which are of direct importance to corrections. In the first, the Court ruled that the ADA's protections extend to inmates.[1] Some lower courts had begun to question if Congress intended the law to apply to inmates, but the Supreme Court settled that question, up to an intriguing point, which leads into the second case. The "point" was a comment the Court made in its "ADA applies to inmates" case, to the effect that the Court was not deciding the question of whether Congress had the power to impose the requirements of the ADA on state governments in the first place.

In its second ADA case, the Supreme Court in 2001 decided that Congress did not have the authority to allow private persons to sue state governments for damages in federal court under the ADA.[2] Thus, in one of the two cases which the Court considered as part of its decision, a security officer who worked for the Alabama Department of Youth Services was barred from seeking damages for what he claimed was the Departments' refusal to meet its duty under the ADA to accommodate disabilities he had.

Like many Supreme Court decisions, the latest one leaves other legal questions unanswered. These questions include whether the portions of the ADA which allow persons to sue for injunctive relief asking that their disabilities be accommodated in some way, and whether the ADA is fully or partially enforceable against units of local government such as cities and counties are valid exercises of congressional power

Until further court decisions clarify the extent to which the ADA applies to state and local governments, one must assume that its general mandates continue to apply, even though damage claims by persons against state governments no longer may be available.

The goal of ADA is to provide a truly equal opportunity for disabled persons to participate in employment and government programs. To do this will require changes in the way employment decisions are made, the way buildings are built, and the way programs are run. For instance, a mobility-impaired person may be able to perform a particular job as well as someone who is fully mobile, except for the fact that the job site is up a flight of stairs that the person cannot climb. To provide the disabled person with an equal opportunity, that physical barrier may have to be removed.

ADA's prohibitions against discrimination are not absolute. In general, a person who is disabled must be "otherwise qualified" to perform the job or participate in a government program or activity. The employer or government service provider must make reasonable accommodations to allow the disabled person to participate, but if the alterations of the job or program would be too great, the individual need not be accommodated. So, the general duty the law creates not to discriminate has limits.

"Disability" is broadly defined under the ADA to include the following:

- A physical or mental impairment that substantially limits one or more of the major life activities of such individual
- A record of such impairment
- Being regarded as having such an impairment

While some may think of ADA as only requiring physical alterations to buildings through such things as ramps, wheelchair lifts, and the like, ADA requires far more than just making a building physically accessible to people in wheelchairs or on crutches. For instance, ADA may require accommodating people with mental disabilities (such as learning disabilities), by making changes in the amount of reading a job or program requires.

While "legitimate penological interests" may permit a correctional institution to restrict the constitutional rights of an inmate (*see* Chapter V), ADA imposes a greater burden on the agency discriminating against a person with a disability to justify that discrimination and avoid accommodating the person's disability in some way. For instance, the employer has a duty to accommodate the otherwise qualified employee with a disability up to the point of the employer incurring an "undue hardship." An undue hardship might be shown if an accommodation were unduly costly, extensive, disruptive, or would fundamentally alter the nature of the operation or business. Note, these are subjective determinations, which will vary from one setting to another. Similar burdens exist to justify denying access to a government program or service. Detailed federal regulations flesh out and interpret the statutory requirements of ADA.[3]

Federal appeals courts are split on the question of whether institutional security concerns can validly justify discriminating against disabled inmates under the ADA and whether the *"Turner* test" (*see* Ch. V) can be used to evaluate this type of issue.[4]

In the *Gates* case, HIV-positive inmates protested being barred from being allowed to work in prison food services. They argued that the bar violated their rights under the ADA. Officials said their decision was based not on a fear that HIV would be transmitted by the inmates, but rather in response to threats of disturbances from other inmates. The district court ruled in favor of the HIV-positive inmates, but the court of appeals reversed, holding that legitimate security needs of the prison justified the exclusion, even though neither ADA nor its regulations recognize security concerns as a basis for discriminating against a person. The court simply created a new exception to the law. Should courts follow the *Gates* approach, it could substantially limit the application of ADA in many prison settings.

Notes

1. In *Pennsylvania Department of Corrections v. Yeskey*, 524 U.S. 206, 118 S.Ct. 1952, 141 L.Ed.2d 215 (1998).
2. *Board of Trustees of the University of Alabama v. Garrett*, ___ S.Ct. ___, 2001 WL 173556 (2001).
3. *See* 28 CFR Parts 25 and 29, CFR Part 1630. The ADA appears at 42 USC Sec. 12020, et. seq.
4. *Gates v. Rowland*, 39 F.3d 1439 (9th Cir., 1994) applied the *Turner* test. But in, *Onishea v. Hopper*, 126 F.3d 1323 (11th Cir., 1997) the court rejected this approach.

Answers to Review Questions

Chapter 2

1. The three periods or eras of court involvement with corrections were (a) the hands-off period; (b) the hands-on period; and (c) the one-hand-on, one-hand-off period.

2. Two factors that led to the courts first becoming involved with correctional issues included (a) the general mood in the country for civil rights reform and (b) poor conditions or poor correctional practices.

3. In passing the Prison Litigation Reform Act, Congress attempted to realize the following goals: the first goal was to make it more difficult for inmates to file civil rights lawsuits in federal court; the second goal was to limit the powers of the federal court in ordering relief in "inmate rights" cases.

4. The Supreme Court is requiring lower courts to show increased deference to the judgment of correctional officers and administrators.

Chapter 3

1. The three types of lawsuits filed most commonly by inmates include (a) civil rights (42 USC Sec. 1983), (b) habeas corpus, and (c) torts.

2. True. A state cannot be sued directly in a civil rights action. Under 42 USC Sec. 1983, the suit must be against a "person," and the state is not a person.

3. A supervisor could be held liable in a civil rights action, even if the supervisor did not take part directly in the actions that led to the suit when the supervisor regularly failed to properly supervise officers' use of excess force despite being aware of such improper use of force; then, the supervisor could be found to have "caused" a civil rights violation. Failure to train officers properly in constitutionally sensitive areas also could be the basis of supervisory liability.

Chapter 4

1. The right of access to the courts is an important part of America's legal system because if someone is not able to obtain access to the courts, they have no way to obtain relief if their rights are being violated.

2. If an inmate is represented by appointed counsel in a criminal case, this is not necessarily sufficient access to the courts because counsel appointed in criminal cases often will not provide additional legal assistance to inmates for civil (noncriminal) matters.

3. The major vulnerability of an access to the courts system which is built around books and other written materials is access for the inmate who cannot read.

Chapter 5

1. The most common institutional concern that may justify restriction of an inmate's constitutional rights is security of the institution.

2. False. The *Turner* test has made it easier to justify restrictions.

3. The institution will lose. To win, the institution must explain in at least some detail why the restriction is related to security. The conclusory response given is insufficient.

Chapter 6

1. The most common justification for restricting inmates' First Amendment rights is security of the institution.

2. If an inmate sends his mother a letter criticizing the warden of the prison, the institution may not refuse to mail this letter because the content of the letter does not threaten security or any other legitimate interest of the institution. Letters may not be censored or rejected simply because they are critical of institution policies or staff.

3. The Supreme Court has been increasing the amount of deference lower courts must show to the judgment of correctional officials but officials still must have a legitimate justification and specify that justification if a restriction is challenged.

Chapter 7

1. Even though the Supreme Court has held that inmates have no expectation of privacy in regard to their cells, a cell search might trigger court intervention if the cell was left in shambles after the search. Then, the otherwise reasonable search could be seen as being done in an unreasonable way.

2. To justify visitor strip searches there must be reasonable suspicion that the visitor is hiding contraband on their person.

3. The most important thing for correctional officers to remember when performing inmate searches is to be professional. Respect the dignity of the inmates while doing searches.

Chapter 8

1. Medical staff, not custody staff should make the decision concerning whether an inmate needs medical care. Custody staff need to be aware of when they may be making, in essence, a medical decision, such as when they refuse to allow an inmate to contact medical staff in the middle of the night.

2. The general areas a court will focus on in a conditions of confinement suit include: personal safety, medical care, sanitation, food service, shelter, and clothing: "basic human needs."

3. Crowding is an important issue in conditions of confinement suits because crowding often results in breakdowns of the facility's ability to meet basic human needs of the inmates.

Chapter 9

1. The two types of legal actions that could be brought following a suicide include: (a) a civil rights action (claiming a violation of a constitutional right) and (b) a tort suit (claiming negligence).

2. The three factual claims most likely to appear in a suicide case include: (a) failure to identify a potentially suicidal inmate, (b) failure to monitor a potentially suicidal inmate, once identified, and (c) failure to properly respond to a suicide attempt once it is discovered.

3. Two examples of where an individual officer's failures could provide the basis for a suicide lawsuit include: (a) failure to complete a suicide screening questionnaire at booking and (b) failure to monitor an inmate according to policy (ten-minute checks, fifteen-minute checks, and so forth).

Chapter 10

1. Deadly force may not be used to protect property.

2. In a constitutional excess force case, the five questions a court will ask include:
(a) What was the need for force to be used?
(b) What was the amount of force used?
(c) What injuries were inflicted?
(d) What was the threat perceived by the reasonable correctional officer?
(e) What efforts to temper the use of force were made?

3. Reasons why detailed use-of-force reports are important include:

(a) they allow the supervisor to evaluate the use of force incident

(b) they allow a court to evaluate the use of force incident

(c) they allow the officer to refresh his or her memory about the details of the incident prior to testifying

(d) they may be able to be introduced into evidence at trial

Chapter 11

1. There are more procedural rights in a parole revocation hearing than a prison or jail disciplinary hearing because the potential loss suffered by the parolee is greater than the potential loss the inmate in custody faces.

2. The difference between procedural and substantive due process is that due process focuses on the process followed to make a particular type of decision. For example: procedural due process must be followed in disciplinary hearings. Substantive due process focuses on the final result or condition, not the process. Examples of substantive due process include conditions of confinement for pretrial detainees and the grounds necessary to involuntarily medicate an inmate.

3. The hearing officer may rely on evidence from a witness whose identity is not disclosed where the hearing officer determines the informant is reliable and the information offered is credible.

Chapter 12

1. An agency is likely to refuse to defend an employee sued by an inmate when the employee acts outside the scope of his or her duties and in bad faith.

2. Types of discovery include: (a) depositions, (b) interrogatories, (c) motions to produce, and (d) requests for admissions.

3. When testifying, witnesses should not try to memorize answers to the lawyers' questions.

Chapter 13

1. Sources of officers' rights include:
   (a) union contracts
   (b) civil service laws
   (c) discrimination laws
   (d) occupational health and safety laws, and
   (e) state and federal constitutional law.

2. False. While sexual discrimination is against the law, so is sexual harassment, which is a form of sexual discrimination.

3. False. Courts have not consistently ruled that random urine testing of correctional officers is an unreasonable search; decisions are mixed as to whether correctional officers may be subject to random urine testing.

About the Author

William C. Collins is an attorney and consultant in Olympia, Washington, specializing in correctional law. A former director of ACA's Correctional Law Project, he is the coeditor and cofounder of the *Correctional Law Reporter*, a bimonthly journal that reviews and discusses legal issues and developments in corrections. He has published two books dealing with correctional law as well as numerous articles. Before entering private practice, Collins worked with the Washington State Attorney General's Office as the first head of their corrections division. With more than twenty-five years of experience, he is generally recognized as one of the country's most knowledgeable attorneys in the corrections law field.